THE INVALUABLE PEARL

BUREAU OF JEWISH EDUCATION
RATNER MEDIA CENTER
Curriculum Materials Collection

CMC   Ghatan, H.E. Yedidiah
234.3   The invaluable pearl:
GHA   the unique status of
            women in Judaism
3643

THE INVALUABLE PEARL

The Unique Status of Women in Judaism

Dr. H. E. Yedidiah Ghatan

Bloch Publishing Company · New York

Copyright © 1986
Dr. H.E. Yedidiah Ghatan

All rights reserved. No part of this book may be used or reproduced, translated, stored in a retrieval system of transmitted in any form or by any means, electronic, mechanical, photocopying, or in any manner whatsoever without written permission of the copyright holder.

Published by Bloch Publishing Co., Inc.
Library of Congress Cataloging-in-Publication Data
Ghatan, H.E. Yedidiah, 1958-
  The invaluable pearl.
  Includes bibliographical references and index.
  1. Women in Judaism I. Title.
BM729.W6G47   1986   296'.088042   85-73454

ISBN O-8197-0502-0

MANUFACTURED IN THE UNITED STATES OF AMERICA

*This work is dedicated to my parents
Zachariah and Channah Ghatan,
whose love, devotion, dedication, and self-sacrifice
for their children and family
have been extraordinary.*

Contents

Dedication	v
Acknowledgment	ix
Acknowledgment of the References	xiii
Foreword	xv
Introduction	xvii

Part One: OUR SPLENDID WOMEN
1. The Women of the Pentateuch — 3
2. The Women of the Book of Prophets — 9
3. The Women of the Scrolls — 14
4. The Talmud and Women — 19
5. The Women of the Talmudic Era — 32

Part Two: WOMEN AND SOME BASIC CONCEPTS IN JUDAISM
1. The Unified Role of Man and Woman — 41
2. The Unique Character of Women — 47
3. The Mission of Human Beings and the Infinite Wisdom of God — 52
4. The Fulfillment of Women in Life — 60
5. The Status of the Jewish Woman — 64

Part Three: WOMEN'S EXEMPTIONS AND OBLIGATIONS IN COMMANDMENTS
1. The Commandments and Women — 85
    a. Tefillin — 88
    b. Tzitzit — 93
    c. Reciting the Shema — 95
    d. The Succah (Tabernacle, Booth) — 96

 2. The Study of the Torah by Women   104
 3. Women and Prayer   113
 4. Women's Testimony   121
 5. Women, Marriage, and Divorce   127

Part Four: THE KEY TO THE CONTINUAL SURVIVAL OF THE JEWS
 1. Jews and Morality   139
 2. Mechitzah (Physical Separation Between Men and Women in the Synagogue)   148
 3. Family Purity   159

Part Five: WOMEN AND REDEMPTION
 1. Jews and the Messianic Era   167
 2. Women's Intuition   170
 3. The Role of Women in Bringing Forth the Redeemers of the Jews   172

Afterword   177
Index   185

Acknowledgment

Let not the wise glorify himself in his wisdom; neither let the mighty man glorify himself in his might; let not the rich glorify himself in his riches. But let him that glorifies himself glory in this, that he understands and knows Me, that I am the Lord who exercises kindness on the earth, for in these things I delight, says the Lord (Jeremiah 9:22-23).

The Almighty is the source of all existence. Everything comes to man from the hands of Heaven; strength, wealth, health, cleverness, etc. With this in mind, I would like to thank the Creator who has always been so gracious to me. I am grateful to Him for giving me this invaluable opportunity, the strength, the understanding, and the time to engage in His Torah. I thank Him for providing me the opportunity to attain the Jewish ideal of ללמוד וללמד "to learn and to teach His Torah." And let me pray, ויהי נעם אדני אלהינו עלינו ומעשה ידינו כוננה עלינו ומעשה ידינו כוננהו "May the pleasantness of my Lord, our God, be upon us. May He establish our handiwork for us; our handiwork, may He establish" (Ps. 90:17).

And that: "May the Lord our God be with us, as He was with our forefathers; let Him not leave us, nor forsake us. That He may incline our hearts to Him, to go in all His ways, and to keep His commandments, and His statutes, and His judgments, which He commanded our forefathers. And may these words of mine, with which I have made supplication before the Lord, be close to the Lord our God, day and night, that He maintain the cause of His servant and the cause of His people Israel, each day's need granted on this day. So that all the peoples of the earth may know that Lord is God; there is none else" (I Kings 8:57-60).

And let it be known that: גלוי וידוע לפניך שלא לכבודי עשיתי ולא לכבוד בית אבא אלא לכבודך שלא ירבו מחלוקת בישראל "It is revealed and known before You that neither for my glory nor for the glory of my father's house have I done this, but for Your glory so that discord may not increase in Israel" (Talmud Megillah 3a).

This work, like many others, has taken years of writing, rewriting, revising and editing. It is with great pleasure and gratitude that the author wishes to express his deep-felt appreciation to the many people who have aided in the process in various ways.

The author can lay no claim to originality for the ideas elucidated herein. ". . . there is nothing new under the sun," (Ecclesiastes 1:9). Thus, some of the ideas were heard by the author, directly and indirectly, from a number of his distinguished teachers and friends.

My thanks go to my teachers at James Striar School of Jewish Studies of Yeshiva University, who with exceptional dedication, as was exemplified by its distinguished director Rabbi Moshe Besdin זצ״ל, taught their students, guided them and inspired them.

I am deeply grateful to my distinguished teacher, Rabbi Dr. Meir Fulda, who as a teacher and a close friend has always been there when needed. I thank him for his many helpful suggestions and ideas pertaining to this work, and for his help in arranging for the evaluation of the manuscript by other qualified sources.

I appreciate my teacher's, Rabbi Dr. Abner Weiss, careful and thorough review of the manuscript and his subsequent very helpful suggestions.

I also appreciate Rav Shimon Schwab's sparing time from his busy schedule to review the manuscript, discuss it with me and suggest new ideas and revisions.

Rabbi Yaakov Weinberg of Ner Israel Rabbinical College was kind enough to take time to review the manuscript, discuss it with me, and suggest new ideas. His sincerity and guidance is much appreciated.

Miss Channie Pollack's suggestions and discussions of the different topics were inspiring and quite helpful; many thanks to her.

Dr. Lawrence Schiffman has been very gracious and in many ways has helped the processing of the manuscript; his ideas and suggestions were invaluable. I remain immensely grateful to him.

Acknowledgment

I would also like to thank the following people for their review of the manuscript and their very helpful suggestions: Miss Yosepha Stapansky ז״ל, an unusual and exceptionally dedicated Jewess, may she rest in peace; Dr. Anne Louise Oaklander; Mrs. Sarah (Naiman) Briet; Miss Susan Levine; Miss Racheline Habousha; Mrs. Susy Tawil; Dr. Stuart Abfel; Dr. John Loike; Dr. David Luchins; Dr. Jerome Parness; Mr. Baruch Eisenberg; Dr. Steven and Mrs. Monica Rosenfeld; Dr. Rabbi Shalom and Mrs. Esther Buchbinder; Rabbi Dr. Melech Schacter, Rabbi Hershel Schacter, and Rabbi Mitchell Serles.

Many thanks to those students of Stern College for Women of Yeshiva University who anonymously undertook the task of reviewing the manuscript and suggesting many constructive and helpful ideas.

Mrs. Hadassah Goldsmith, a close friend of the family, was gracious enough to devoutedly spend many hours reviewing and editing the initial draft of the manuscript. I am indebted to her for her valuable contributions and suggestions.

The staff members of Computer Center of the Albert Einstein College of Medicine of Yeshiva University, and Mr. Oded Lion and Mr. Robert Berlinger, in particular, were very helpful in the processing of the manuscript.

The special and exceptional friendship and encouragement of the following people have been a great source of inspiration for the author: Dr. Raphael Moller זצ״ל; Mr. and Mrs. John Rothschild; Mr. and Mrs. Fred Wurzburger; Mr. and Mrs. Eric Katzenstein; Mr. and Mrs. Eric Hess; Mr. and Mrs. Dov Kurland. I sincerely thank them all.

Many thanks to my faithful roommates whose friendly discussions inspired me with new ideas. Thanks to Dr. Hillel Rosen, Dr. Stuart Kaplan, Mr. Adam Karp, and Mr. Jeffrey Feldman.

Members of my family, Mr. Nissan and Mrs. Leah Kaverah; Mr. Uriel and Mrs. Rivka Golfiz; and Miss Sarah Ghatan helped me in various ways in the processing and publishing of this work—my heartfelt thanks to them all.

Special thanks is due to the Bloch Publishing Company—Mr. Charles Bloch, Mrs. Susan Cizma. And special appreciation to Mrs. Mindy Leaf for her writing, rewriting, and editorial skills.

Therefore, whatever merit may pertain to this work, the author gladly shares it with all of those mentioned; shortcomings are his alone.

ידידיה קטן
תשמ"ו

Acknowledgment of The References

The author acknowledges with gratitude permission to reprint excerpts from the following works:

Rabbi Samson Raphael Hirsch, *The Pentateuch* (Judaica Press, 1982).
Dayan Dr. I. Grunfeld, *Judaism Eternal* (Soncino Press, 1956).
Baruch Litvin, *The Sanctity of Synagogue* (Baruch Litvin Foundation, 1959).
A.E. Kitov, *The Jew And His Home* (Shengold Publishers, Inc., N.Y., 1963).
Rabbi Abraham Besdin, *The Reflections of The Rav* (Jewish Agency, 1979).
Dr. Moshe Meiselman, *Jewish Woman in Jewish Law* (Ktav Publishing House, 1978).
Rabbi Norman Lamm, *A Hedge of Roses* (Rabbi Norman Lamm and Feldheim Publishers, N.Y., 1977).
Rabbi Samson Raphael Hirsch, *The Psalms* (Feldheim Publishers, N.Y., 1966).
Rabbi Samson Raphael Hirsch, *The Siddur* (Feldheim Publishers, N.Y., 1978).

Foreword

Let us begin with the wise words of Rabbi Moshe ben Maiman (known as Rambam or Maimonides) that appear in his introduction to *The Guide for The Perplexed*. "G-d the exalted knows I greatly feared to write of the matters I wished this work to contain... But I rely on two precedents: First, in similar cases our Sages applied the verse, עת תורתך הפרו לה׳ לעשות "It is time to work for the Lord [for] they have made void Your Torah" (Ps. 119:126); secondly, they said: "Let all your deeds be done for the sake of Heaven" (Mishnah Abot 2:12).

The author finds no better way to start this work since I, too, share the views of the Rambam. The author also considers this a personal obligation under the biblical imperative, ואהבת לרעך כמוך "You shall love your neighbor as yourself" (Lev. 19:18). We are all connected to each other like a large chain and, therefore, responsible for one another. כל ישראל ערבין זה בזה "All Jews are responsible for one another" (Sanhedrin 27b, Shavuot 39a).

Introduction

The status and role of women in Judaism are two of the most vital issues facing the Jewish world today. Living in a foreign and secular culture, it is only natural to be influenced by the values of that culture, and those of us who have not had the opportunity to fully appreciate the beauty, justice, understanding, and vast knowledge contained in the Jewish tradition and law, often misunderstand the true essence of this majestic heritage.

In recent years, the feminist movement has raised a number of questions concerning the way women are treated under Jewish law. This book attempts to demonstrate that women do not hold an inferior position in Jewish life but, on the contrary, Judaism assigns women a role of singular importance and honor.

The book is divided into five parts. *Part One,* an overview of the splendid women of the Bible and Talmud, also serves as background for some of the themes developed later on in the book.

Part Two defines a number of topics, and sets the stage for an extensive discussion of the status of the Jewish woman found towards the end of the chapter.

The exemption of women from certain "time-bound positive commandments" is covered in *Part Three.* Questions pertaining to women being counted as part of a *minyan* (a quorum for public prayers), women's testimony, marriage and divorce are also reviewed in this part.

Part Four discusses morality—as it concerns the Jews in particular and the world at large. In this context, *mechitzah* (the physical separation between men and women in synagogues) is explained. Also discussed are a number of rationales for the laws of family purity.

It is beyond the scope of any book to cover every question a reader might have regarding the position of women in Judaism. Therefore, this book concentrates on addressing those items which have become major sources of misunderstanding. "Derogatory" and "unfavorable" remarks found in the Talmud concerning women; grouping of women with minors, slaves, etc.; singing of women in the presence of men; and women and careers are all examples of issues discussed.

In addition, a number of key principles are developed which will hopefully prove helpful to the reader in answering questions that are not specifically addressed in this work.

The reader is urged to read the book in a sequential manner, since many of the themes and concepts appearing later in the volume refer to discussions and principles clarified earlier on.

In order to accomodate readers of all backgrounds, an effort has been made to translate and explain the Hebrew quotes cited.

Although this book deals basically with women in Judaism, it is hoped that both women *and* men will find it to be a source of valuable information and inspiration.

Part One
OUR SPLENDID WOMEN

Part One presents a chronological account of the deeds of noble women in Jewish history. The purpose of this presentation is twofold: First, to relate the accomplishments and status of these women, including their function as role-models; and second, to serve as background material for some of the concepts explored later on in the book.

1

The Women of the Pentateuch

Our rich tradition is replete with accounts of the contributions made by our women. Let us review a number of instances that testify to the superior spirituality, intelligence, understanding and judgement of women in our history. We can start at the beginning with the mother of prophecy—our mother Sarah, the wife of Abraham.

In chapter 16 of the book of Genesis we are told that Sarah was barren, she had no children. However, she felt "... maybe I shall be built up through her" (referring to her handmaid, Hagar) (Gen. 16:2). So she urged her husband Abraham to marry her Egyptian handmaid, Hagar, so that he might beget a child through her. The Bible informs us of Abraham's reaction to this unusual request, "And Abraham hearkened to the voice of Sarai" (Ibid). Rashi, the most famous and authoritative biblical commentator, quotes the Genesis Rabbah in his explanation that Abraham listened to the *Holy Spirit* that was within his wife. This was an indication of Sarah's spiritual superiority over Abraham.

Likewise, it was Sarah who noticed the unbecoming behavior of Ishmael (the subsequent son of Hagar and Abraham), and perceived the destruction it might cause. So she said to Abraham, "Cast out this bondwoman and her son; for he shall not be heir, the son of this bondwoman with my son, with Isaac" (Gen. 21:10). This filled Abraham with great grief and indecision until God said to him: "All that Sarah says to you listen to her voice" (Gen. 21:12). Rashi comments that from here we learn that Abraham was inferior to Sarah in prophecy.

Later on in the Bible, Rebecca, Isaac's wife, demonstrated her superior understanding and judgement when Isaac was about to give "the special blessing" (of the patriarch's) to his favorite son Esau. Rebecca very shrewdly counseled *her* favorite son, the righteous Jacob, to get "the special blessing" from his father Isaac, in place of his unworthy brother Esau.

Rachel, the most beloved wife of Jacob, has become the symbol of the distressed Jewish nation. She was the one who pleaded before God to have mercy on her children when they were driven into exile out of the land of Israel. As we find in Jeremiah 31:14-16:

> Thus says the Lord:
> A voice is heard in Ramah
> Lamentation and bitter weeping
> Rachel weeping for her children
> She refuses to be comforted for her children
> Because they are not.
> Thus says the Lord:
> Refrain your voice from weeping
> And your eyes from tears
> For your work shall be rewarded, says the Lord.
> And they shall come back to the land of the enemy
> And there is hope for your future, says the Lord.
> And your children shall return to their own borders.

Rachel had shown herself to be self-sacrificing and concerned about others much before then. When Laban the Aramian agreed to the marriage of his daughter Rachel to Jacob, both Rachel and Jacob knew full well that Laban was not honest enough to keep his word. To prevent being tricked, they chose a secret password to use on their wedding night—a word that would let Jacob know it was indeed

Rachel under the thick veil. Laban was deceitful, arranging for his older daughter Leah to marry Jacob in Rachel's place. Rachel discovered Laban's plans, but couldn't face publicly shaming her sister, so she told her the secret password (Rashi quoting Genesis Rabbah on Gen. 30:22). Thus, we learn from Rachel's example, the ultimate attributes of selflessness, and self-sacrifice.

Leah is credited in the Talmud Berachot 7b as the first human being who offered praises to the Lord. ". . . this time will I praise the Lord . . ." (Gen. 29:35). Leah was so meritorious that she was blest with having all the kings of Judea, including King David and King Solomon and prophets such as Moses, Samuel, and Isaiah, descend from her line.

Another very wise woman of the Bible was Sarach, the daughter of Asher (Asher was one of Jacob's twelve sons). When Jacob's sons returned from Egypt with the knowledge that their brother Joseph was alive and well, they did not know how to break the good news to their father without shocking him to death. So they approached Sarach for advice. It was she who in her superior wisdom decided to chant with music "Joseph is still alive, Joseph is still alive," thereby gently letting Jacob grow accustomed to the idea. When Jacob later learned of this wise act of Sarach, he blessed her with everlasting life (Meam Loez on Gen. 45:25).

Yet another instance. When God wished to remind Israel of the acts of kindness He had shown them, He spoke to them through the prophet Micah. The first act God mentions is the appointment of Moses, Aaron, and Miriam as leaders of the people. It was Miriam who was chosen to be the leader of the Jewish women at the time of the exodus and during their wanderings in the desert, just as her brothers Moses and Aaron, were chosen to lead the men. From this it is apparent that Miriam held equal rank with our great leaders, Moses and Aaron. And the Talmud Tannit 9a testifies to this fact by stating that three good leaders stood for Israel—Moses, Aaron, and Miriam.

More testimony to women's superior spirituality in biblical times, is the quote we often hear during Passover: בשכר נשים צדקנית שהיו באתו הדור נגאלו ישראל ממצרים "Due to the merit of the righteous women of that generation, Israel was redeemed from Egypt" (Sotah 11b).

During the Egyptian slavery, when pharaoh decreed that all male children born to Jews be thrown into the Nile, the Jewish men thought to prevent the certain death of their children by abstaining from relations with their wives. The meritorious and courageous women living during that time then deliberately set about making themselves as attractive as possible so that their husbands would return to them. In order to accomplish this, the women used mirrors and other beauty aids. [Interestingly, many years later when the children of Israel were commanded to build the sanctuary in the desert, one of the first vessels they were asked to make was the kiyor (laver), which was constructed of these very same mirrors. The mirrors symbolized the women's faith in God and their devotion to their husbands. It is even more interesting to note that these vessels were used to hold water, a symbol of life and purity.]

Contrary to the men's rationalization for separating from their wives, the women strongly desired to bear children against all odds for their survival. It was the goal of these righteous women to bear children, raise them, and transmit to them their faith in God. During all the torturous years of slavery in Egypt, these women underwent great sacrifices for the sake of raising a nation. Therefore, it is not surprising that our rabbis of blessed memory said, "Each generation is redeemed because of the righteous women of that generation."

When Moses was late in coming down from the mountain with the ten commandments, the children of Israel decided to build an idol—a golden calf—to lead them. Consequently, the women were asked to surrender their jewels to be used for making the golden calf, but they refused. The men had to exert force to get the jewels away from them. Because these women of Israel demonstrated such extraordinary piety and fear of God, they were later given *Rosh Hodesh,* the beginning of the month, as an optional holiday.

There are a number of reasons offered as to why *Rosh Hodesh,* and not any other holiday, was especially associated with women. The *Orah Hachaim* 417 writes that the holidays are associated with the forefathers: Passover with Abraham, Pentecost with Isaac, and Succoth with Jacob. And the twelve *Roshei Hodeshim* were originally meant to be associated with the twelve tribes. But since the men sinned with the golden calf, it was taken from them and was associated with their wives—who did not participate in the sin—instead.

Or Zarua 2:454 suggests that just like every month a woman goes through her cycle and becomes new and immerses herself (in the waters of the *mikvah*) and returns to her husband and is dear to him as the day of their marriage; so, too, the moon goes through cycles and becomes new and everybody wishes to see it. Thus it is only befitting that women who share this common characteristic with the moon be given *Rosh Hodesh* as a holiday.

While in the wilderness, the men repeatedly rebelled against God and His prophets, Moses and Aaron. Their rebellious slogan was "Let us appoint a leader and go back to Egypt." The women, on the other hand, were God-fearing, righteous, and faithful. Their slogan was "Give us an inheritance [in the land of Israel]" (Rashi on Numb. 26:64). When God wanted to punish the Israelites for their rebelliousness, He decreed that that generation would not enter the Holy Land. This decree excluded, however, these faithful and God-fearing women (Ibid).

Among the women of the Pentateuch, the four daughters of Zelophehad stand out as *hachmaniot,* (scholars). When Moses was discussing the laws of levirate marriage, the daughters of Zelophehad approached him to ask if they had the right to inherit land in Israel since their father had died leaving no sons. Moses brought the case before God, and God said to Moses: "The daughters of Zelophehad speak right: thou shall surely give them a possession of an inheritance among their father's brethren; and thou shall cause to pass the inheritance of their father unto them" (Num. 27:7). Rashi comments that this section of the Torah was worthy of being written by Moses, but since the daughters of Zelophehad were found worthy as well, it was written through them. He adds that The-Holy-One-Blessed-be-He said: "Thus this section is written before Me in the heavens," indicating that the eyes of the daughters of Zelophehad saw what the eyes of Moses did not see. Furthermore, in the Talmud it is stated that the fact that the daughters of Zelophehad brought their case before Moses at the same time he was discussing the laws of the levirate marriage proves that they were scholars.

2
The Women of the Book of Prophets

Deborah the prophetess was a woman in our ancient history who guided the destiny of the Jewish people during the time of the Judges. It was through the leadership of Deborah, that the people of Israel prevailed over Yabin, the king of Canaan, who had oppressed the Jews for twenty years.

Deborah's husband was ignorant; therefore she made wicks for him to bring to the Sanctuary and thereby merit the World to Come. In connection with this the Sages said, "The wisdom of a woman builds a man's house." Deborah made thick wicks, like torches, to emit a great deal of light. The-Holy-One-Blessed-be-He then said that because she intended to increase His light, He would cause her light to shine over Israel (see *Yalkut Shimoni* on Shoftim 4).

Deborah is referred to as a judge in the Scripture. Although according to Jewish law a woman may not be a judge, nevertheless, Deborah was accepted as such under Divine instruction. An alternate explanation would be that she did not actually judge, but merely publicized the laws. (See Tosfot on Gittin 88b.) *Aruch ha-Shulchan Choshen Mishpat* 7:4 suggests that when it comes to money matters, litigants may accept anyone's judgement (i.e. even a woman's).

Since women cannot be witnesses (reasons for this will be elaborated further on in the section on Women's Testimony), they may not judge either. However, Ritva and Rabbenu Tam are both of the opinion that they can be judges in the manner of biblical Deborah. Others agree, but limit a women's ability to be a judge. Still others argue that Deborah was not a judge herself, but rather guided the people and instructed and directed the judges.

Tanna de be Eliyahu asks: "What was so special about Deborah to deserve to be a judge and a prophetess in Israel? Was not Pinhas son of Elazar alive yet (and therefore more deserving to assume such a high position)? But I call upon heaven and earth to witness, be it a gentile or a Jew, a man or a woman, a manservant or a maidservant, the spirit of God rests upon him (her) only according to his (her) deeds."

The manner in which the Bible relates Deborah's victory and refers to her position as a judge proves that there was no public prejudice against a woman, provided she was a capable leader.

Another woman of exceptional bravery and wisdom was Yael, a contemporary of Deborah's. Her heroic action is recorded in the fourth chapter of the Book of Judges. Upon being pursued by the victorious Israelites, Sisera, a mighty adversary, fled on foot to the tent of Yael, the wife of Heber the Kenite. Yael went out to Sisera and invited him into her tent. When Sisera asked her for some water, she instead gave him to drink from a flask of milk. Afterwards, while he was in a deep sleep, she ". . . took the tent-pin and placed the hammer in her hand, and came to him steadily, and thrust the pin into his temple, and it pierced through into the ground, and he was in a deep sleep and weary; and he died" (Judges. 4:21). And thus Yael helped bring about a short period of tranquility to the constantly oppressed Israelites during the time of the Judges.

Channah is celebrated as the Jewish mother *par excellence*. The fact that we read the story of Channah on *Rosh Hashanah* (the Jewish New Year) testifies to her importance. To celebrate the festivals three times a year, Channah and her husband, Elkanah, made a pilgrimage to the sanctuary of God in Shiloh. They were also instrumental in bringing their fellow Jews closer to God by encouraging them to join in these pilgrimages.

Despite all her accomplishments, Channah felt a deep void in her life because she was childless. The Bible relates that once, while in Shiloh, she prayed most sincerely before God for a son and vowed that if her wishes were granted, she would consecrate her child's entire life to the service of God. While she was praying, Eli, the high priest, noticed that her lips were moving but no words were being uttered. He therefore presumed the woman was drunk. However, when he looked at the wings of the cherubs (two winged celestial objects in the form of winged children facing each other on the ark in the Holy Temple) and saw them move—a sign that Channah's prayers were being accepted—Eli, too, blessed her and prayed that her prayers would be answered in full (1 Samuel 1:17).

The Talmud Berachot 31b credits Channah as being the first to address God as צבאות ("Master of Legions"). At Shiloh she prayed before the Lord saying, "Master of Legions, of all the hosts of heaven that You created in Your world, would it be unpleasing to You to give me a son?"

Channah's prayer was answered. She later gave birth to Samuel, the last of the judges and one of the greatest prophets. He was so great a prophet that our sages said that Samuel in his generation was on par with Moses in his generation.

Deborah's song of victory and Channah's prayer of thankfulness are perhaps the noblest outpourings of love for God that adorn the national literature of the Jewish people.

Throughout the ages, women have used their intuitive wisdom and understanding to influence men in high office. The following narratives serve as examples.

After King David's handsome son, Abshalom, killed his brother, Amnon, the king banished him from the court. Three years passed, and David found himself longing for his banished son, but he would not call him back. Thereupon, Yoab, commander-in-chief of the king's army, found a "wise woman" to persuade David to send for Abshalom. By using an appropriate parable, the wise woman managed to admonish the king and convince him to send for his son.

Another "wise woman" of the time was influential in preventing Yoab from destroying the city of Abel Beth-Maakha. Yoab and his army were holding the city in siege because a rebel against King David had found refuge there. The following words which the "wise woman" said to Yoab illustrate her genuine concern for her city, and her proud, motherly love. "I am of [those] that are peaceful and faithful to Israel. Do you seek to destroy a city and a mother in Israel? Why will you swallow up the inheritance of the Lord?" (II Samuel 20:19). This wise woman then devised a plan for delivering the rebel's head to Yoab. The head was "delivered" and Yoab promptly withdrew his forces from the city.

The narrative of Ritzpah (II Samuel 21) illustrates just how powerful the feminine traits of motherly love and understanding truly are. It happened that a terrible famine raged throughout Israel during King David's reign. When David consulted the *Urim Ve-Tumim* (the Divine Oracle), he was told that the famine was divine punishment for cruelties committed against the Gibeonites by King Saul. In order to make amends for Saul's crimes, David gave seven of Saul's grandsons to the Gibeonites to do with as they pleased. The Gibeonites hung all seven and, to add insult, left their bodies lying in the open, unburied. Still the famine in Israel did not cease. It was only when Ritzpah (the mother of two of Saul's slain grandsons), acting out of motherly love and superior understanding, covered the bodies of the seven dead men with sackcloth, that events took a turn. David was so moved by Ritzpah's pious action that he arranged for a proper funeral for the bones of those who had been hanged. He was also reminded to arrange for Saul and Jonathan to be properly eulogized. And only then did the famine cease. Thus we see how even King David was humbly ready to learn from the examples of a tender, wise, and good-hearted woman.

Another woman of unique stature during the biblical period was Huldah the prophetess, a contemporary of the prophet Jeremiah. While repairing the Temple under the direction of King Josiah, a Scroll of Law was found in the House of the Lord. After reading the scroll, the king became very troubled and sent for the prophetess Huldah to verify it. The Sages disagree as to the reason why Huldah, not the prophet Jeremiah, was contacted. According to one opinion, it was because women are more merciful than men. The king sent for Huldah hoping that she would pray that all the bad decrees found in the Scroll of Law would not come upon the kingdom and his people.

Zephaniah, Huldah and Jeremiah were the only prophets of that particular generation. It was said that Jeremiah prophesied in the streets, Zephaniah prophesied in the synagogues, and Huldah prophesied to the women.

3
The Women of the Scrolls

One of the most famous women of Jewish history is Queen Esther. According to the Megillah, Esther was an orphan raised by her uncle Mordechai. In Talmud Megillah 13a, however, our Sages teach that she was married to Mordechai. When King Achashverosh sought a wife, his agents took Esther to the King's harem by force. (For a halachic discussion of the questions raised by this issue, the reader is referred to Talmud Sanhedrin 74b and Ketubot 57b).

Earlier, Esther had tried every possible means to avoid being abducted, but to no avail. Both Esther and Mordechai had a prophetic vision that led them to understand that all that happened was part of a Divine master-plan to bring redemption to the Jews at a later date.

Esther exhibited exceptional self-sacrifice and devotion in Achashverosh's court. Though surrounded by heathens, she kept her national identity a secret and observed God's commandments in private. We can appreciate the depths of Esther's ordeal from her prayer to God as she prepared to break the king's law by appearing unbidden to beg Ahashverosh for the survival of her fellow Jews.

> My God, my God, why have You forsaken me? Why have You changed the order of the world and the order of the Jewish mothers against me? Sarah was taken captive by Pharaoh for one night and he and his household were punished. I have been placed in the bosom of this evil man for so many years and no

miracles have helped me. Jewish women have three special commandments, and I keep them even here. Why have You forsaken me? (Midrash Shocher Tov 22:26).

Afterwards, Queen Esther daringly and cunningly exposed the wicked Haman, a high officer in King Achashverosh's court, who had plotted to kill all the Jews within the confines of the Persian Empire. She was able to void the decree that would have killed, in one day, all the Jews living in that land. It is in commemoration of this miraculous event, that we fast every year on the thirteenth day of the month of *Adar,* and then celebrate Purim and read the Megillah of Esther (the Book of Esther) in the synagogues on the next day. The fast itself is called "The Fast of Esther" in honor of this courageous Jewess.

The Megillah of Ruth (the Book of Ruth), which we read in the synagogues on the holiday of Shavuot (the Pentecost), has a housewife and mother as its central figure. Ruth did not play a role in public life, but rather was an ordinary woman, devoted to her husband and family. She found her ideals and life's goals within the narrow confines of her household. Yet this simple mother and housewife was found worthy enough to be the ancestor of the great King David. We are told the Messiah will also be a descendant of Ruth.

The Book of Ruth tells the story of Elimelech, his wife Naomi, and their two sons, who settled in Moab in order to escape the famine in Judah. In Moab, the boys married Moabite girls, but within a short time the two young husbands and their father Elimelech died. Helpless and lonely, Naomi decided to return to her native Bethlehem in Judah. Her two Moabite daughters-in-law, Orpah and Ruth, decided to accompany her. But when Naomi described the joyless and dreary life awaiting them in Judah, Orpah turned back to Moab. Ruth, however, refused to forsake her mother-in-law, entreating her to let her come with her to Judah. She said:

... wherever you go, I will go; wherever you stay, I will stay; your people shall be my people, and your God shall be my God, ...

Ruth followed Naomi to Bethlehem where she devotedly cared for her for the rest of her days. Ruth's devotion to Naomi was so special that the townspeople considered her to be better to her mother-in-law "than seven sons" (Ruth 4:15).

What was so special about Ruth that she deserved to have David, and later the Messiah, to descend from her? True altruism is almost impossible to achieve; however, this is a highly desired trait in Jewish theology. For example, the most cherished way to dispense charity is when the person who is giving the charity does not know to whom he is giving it, and the person receiving the charity does not know from whom he is receiving it. Charity, good deeds, done on behalf of a dead person is in the highest category of charities, חסד של אמת. Such altruistic charity is what distinguish Ruth and Tamar (for the story of Tamar see Gen. 38), as the *Zohar* teaches us: "There were two women from whom were built the seed of Judah and from whom descended King David, King Solomon, and the King Messiah . . . Tamar and Ruth . . . Both acted properly in order to do good with the dead."

This simple tale of love and devotion teaches us an ethical lesson, and has been a source of inspiration throughout the ages. As Rabbi Zeira emphasizes in *Yalkut Shimoni* on Ruth, "This Megillah [Ruth] does not contain laws of purity and impurity, neither prohibition nor permissibility. And why was it written? To teach us how much good deeds are meritorious."

The story of Chanukah is not biblical. However, because it pertains to the accomplishments of the women of the same period, it is included here. Briefly, the holiday of Chanukah commemorates two events:

(1) The military victory, in 165 B.C.E., of a small Jewish army, the Maccabees, against the vast forces of the Syrian-Macedonian empire. The ruling Syrian-Greeks attempted to suppress Judaism and the study and practice of the Torah. They defiled the Holy Temple and prompted the worship of the Hellenic deities. The Maccabee victory restored the free practice of Judaism and regained a measure of political independence for the Jews.

(2) A symbolic ritual miracle accompanied the military miracle. Eager to resume the Temple service, the Maccabees wished to rekindle the lights of the Temple *Menorah* (candelabra). A search of the Temple storehouse uncovered just one intact flask of ritually pure oil—enough to keep the Menorah lit for only one day. However, the oil miraculously burned for eight days, until new pure oil could be prepared.

In remembrance of these events we celebrate Chanukah by lighting candles for eight nights in a row. We also add special prayers of thanksgiving to our daily prayers during this time.

A closer look at history reveals the crucial role brave and righteous women of the period played in instigating rebellion against our oppressors.

Ignoring strict Syrian prohibitions against all religious activities, these virtuous women continued to circumcise their sons. Then to arouse their husbands (who were hiding from the Syrians) to revolution, they climbed the walls of Jerusalem and leapt to their deaths with their sons in their arms. The women's message to their husbands was clear. If the men did not have the courage to fight against the enemy, neither their wives nor their children would remain.

The unheard of sacrifice of these heroic women later served as a great source of encouragement and inspiration to the men who heeded their message, went to battle against the Syrians, and defeated them.

One last note of female heroism. History has it that the governor of the land at the time was enamored with the daughter of Mattityahu, the high priest, and took her to his palace. There, Mattityahu's daughter fed him wine and cheese in order to get him drunk. When the man was in a stupor, she then very daringly cut off his head and brought it with her to Jerusalem. The woman's brave deed is said to have served as an encouragement for the Jews to revolt. (There are various versions of this event. Some sources say the act was committed by a widow named Yehudit).

Because of this story, some people keep the custom of eating cheese during Chanukah. And since women were centrally involved in the miracle of Chanukah, many women have a tradition of not doing any work while the flames burn in the menorah.

4
The Talmud and Women

The term *Torah* refers to two entities—the written and the unwritten law—both of which were revealed to Moses at Mount Sinai (see Rashi on Lev. 26:46). The written law consists of the five books of the Pentateuch, herein referred to as the Torah. The unwritten (oral) law consists of expositions and interpretations which were communicated to Moses orally as a supplement to the written law. Without the oral law, the scriptural texts would often be unintelligible since many seem contradictory. The oral law, also known as the *Talmud,* is further explained below.

The word Talmud literally means "the study." The Talmud is a many-volumed work written partly in Hebrew and partly in Aramaic. The volumes are divided into two distinct portions: the *Mishnah* and the *Gemara.*

There are differences of opinions as to the derivation and meaning of the word *Mishnah.* Some scholars hold that it is derived from the word שנה "shanah" which means "to teach orally," referring to the fact that it was transmitted from generation to generation by word-of-mouth. Other authorities hold that the word *Mishnah* has the same root as the word שנים "shnaim" meaning "two," which signifies that the Mishnah is *second* in rank to the Torah.

The Mishnah was compiled and edited by Rabbi Yehuda Hanasi who died about the end of the second century of the common era. The Mishnah is made up of six sections, one of which is entitled "Women." The fact that an entire section is devoted to women points to the great importance assigned to the Jewish woman in Jewish law.

The word *Gemara* is derived from the word גמר "gemar." In Hebrew גמר means "to complete," hence some authorities hold that the word Gemara means "completion of" or "supplement to" the *Mishnah*. In Aramaic, however, the word גמר means "to teach," and hence other authorities hold that the word *Gemara* has the same meaning as the word *Talmud*, i.e. "the teaching," or "the study."

The *Gemara*, which consists of commentaries on the *Mishnah*, is the sum total of legal analytical discussions of the sages (the rabbis), who were the spiritual leaders of Judaism, extending during a course of approximately eight centuries (300 B.C.E. to 500 C.E.).

Scholars at the time of the Gemara were known as *Amoraim*. They resided in two distinct locations—Babylon and Palestine. Each location had its own particular way of expounding on the Mishnah that was somewhat different from the other. Hence, we have two compilations of the Gemara. The *Talmud Babli*—or Babylonian Talmud—compiled by Rabbi Ashi, the president of the academy of Sura, and Rabbi Yosi, the president of the academy of Pumbeditha; and the *Talmud Yerushalmi*—or the Palestinian Talmud—compiled in the academies of Palestine.

The Babylonian Talmud is a much more extensive and analytical work than the Palestinian Talmud. Thus, it is the one more widely studied and utilized to expound Jewish law. Henceforth in this book, the word "Talmud" will refer to the Babylonian Talmud unless otherwise specified.

The Talmud is the central focus of the Jewish legal system, a system distinguished by a marked relationship between law and ethics. It embodies religious beliefs, religious laws, and worldly wisdom. It also devotes much space to the discussion of the legal (halachic) status and social position of women in the Jewish faith. Biographies of distinguished women of the Talmudic era occasionally grace its pages as well.

Thus the Talmud is far more than a collection of legal decisions. Its subject matter is so vast and its teachings so deep, that a person who desires to familiarize himself with the intricacies of this gigantic work needs the help of expert guides. These guides would clarify not only the methods and terminology employed, and particularly grammatical language, but they would also consider the traditional and historical development of Talmudic law which, for all practical purposes, has the same authoritative character as the written law (Torah).

The Talmud is packed with interesting anecdotes, maxims, proverbs, history, theology, mathematics, biology, philosophy, medicine, geography, and jurisprudence. What makes the Talmud even more uniquely fascinating is the fact that it is not a conventional or simplified anthology of unanimous opinions. On the contrary, it is a document filled with the most extreme contradictions, as is life itself. Nevertheless, the Talmud's aim is to regulate and give order to life ... it is the main source from which Jewish law springs.

Here it should be emphasized that each opinion, by itself, retains its own merit, regardless of the fact that it seems to be contradicted by another opinion. In fact, often when two seemingly contradictory opinions are discussed at length in the Talmud, it becomes apparent that there is indeed no contradiction. Some minute detail—that was not taken into account—had caused the reader to assume a contradiction where none existed. The appearance of contradictions is a major factor in what makes the Talmud so complex, yet so rewarding, fulfilling, and satisfying when understood in the correct perspective, and learned in the proper framework.

The richness and diversity of the Talmud is an apt reflection of its authors. Among contributors, we find rich and poor, aristocrats and day-laborers, urbanites and villagers. This may, to some extent, explain the many contradictory statements and differences of opinion found therein. And one can, perhaps, also better understand why statements expressing the highest regard and admiration for women appear alongside unfavorable remarks. Can the reason for such contradictory statements simply lie in the fact that the authors were influenced by their personal experience with females?

Rabbi Eliezer Ben Hyrkanos, the husband of the intellectually gifted Ima Shalom, expresses the following opinions in the Talmud Sotah 20a: "He who teaches his daughter the Law is as if he taught her frivolity." Is it possible that Rabbi Eliezer's personal experience with his smart wife turned him into a steadfast opponent of women's education?

On the other hand, Ben Azzai expresses the following opinion: "Every parent is obligated to instruct his daughter in Torah."

Such contradictory opinions might make it look like the Talmudists were not absolutely free from human shortcomings . . . and that they let their personal experiences influence their outlook on life. This is not necessarily the case, however, as will be evident from the following discussion. The seemingly contradictory statements made by Rabbi Eliezer and Ben Azzai could be resolved as follows. When Rabbi Eliezer says "the Law," he is referring only to the Talmud. He has no objection to women learning or being taught Jewish precepts in order to know how to conduct their lives, or to women learning or being taught the Bible. Therefore, Ben Azzai's opinion on "teaching Torah" to women is compatible with Rabbi Eliezer's opinion. (The topic of Torah study for women will be dealt with in detail later on.)

Another aspect of the Talmud which makes it a highly complex work, sometimes difficult to comprehend and at times misleading, is its code words and phrases which obviously cannot and should not be understood literally (but only figuratively). For the most part, the true connotation of these code words and phrases has been taught from master to student throughout Jewish history. Some of these oral communications have been lost to us, but fortunately many are known.

First, let us clarify by whose authority our rabbis of-blessed-memory interpreted and derived laws from the Torah. God Himself decreed: "According to the law which they shall teach you, and according to the judgement which they shall tell you, you shall do, you shall not turn aside from the word which they shall declare to you (neither to the right nor to the left)" (Deut. 17:11). The above verse can be read as an explicit biblical sanction authorizing our rabbis who are knowledgeable and well-versed in the Torah and in all that pertains to it, to make necessary enactments to safeguard and promote the Torah among the Jews. In Lev. 18:30 we read, ". . . you should safeguard that which I have placed in your charge." The Talmud Moed Katan 5a and Yebamot 21a explain it means that you should make provisions to safeguard the observance of the Torah, that is, enact measures to protect the laws of Torah from being violated. The rabbis' enactments, however, must be made in accordance with already-set precedents of the Torah; the rules of interpretation of the Torah which were revealed to Moses and from Moses transmitted orally from generation to generation (e.g. the hermeneutic principles). (Note: "Hermeneutic principles" refer to the principles of interpretation of the Torah handed down to Moses at Sinai.)

Anybody who disobeys the rabbinic enactments transgresses two biblical commandments implied in Deut. 17:11: The positive commandment—to do in accordance with what the rabbis teach us, and the negative commandment—not to turn aside from what they teach us.

The extent and nature of the authority vested in the rabbis is highly impressive. To illustrate: In the Talmud Baba Metzia 59b we find the famous discussion around the *Aknai Oven*. The subject matter was a question of ritual purity. The majority of the sages sharply disagreed with the mighty Rabbi Eliezer, who surpassed them all in piety. To prove the rightness of his opinion, Rabbi Eliezer called for a number of miracles to occur. However, the sages were not impressed by the miracles and stuck to their original argument. Finally, a heavenly voice announced that Rabbi Eliezer's opinion was correct. Upon hearing the heavenly voice, Rabbi Yehoshua stood up and responded, "It is not in the heavens."

The Talmud interprets Rabbi Yehoshua's statement by maintaining that the Torah was already given to us from Mount Sinai, and from generation to generation the rules, methods, and principles of interpretation of the Torah have been handed down through the rabbis. The Torah gives us permission to make decisions in accordance with the opinion of the majority. Thus halacha can only be decided based on proofs and refutations of the sages in this world: "It is not in the heavens"—a heavenly voice and other heavenly signs are not acceptable.

Not only are the decisions of our sages sanctioned by Divine Law, but the sages also enjoy Divine supervision while making such decisions, as we learn in Mishnah Abot 3:6:

> Rabbi Halafta ben Dosa of Kfar Hananya said: When ten people sit together and occupy themselves with the Torah, the *Shechinah* (Divine Presence) resides among them, as it is said: "God stands in the godly congregation" (Ps. 82:1). [Note: "Congregation" is the word used for ten males.] Whence do we know that the same applies to five? It is said: "He has founded his association upon the earth" (Amos 9:6). [Note: The Hebrew word אגודה "association" refers to what one can gather in one hand—which has five fingers—thus association connotes a group of five.] Whence do we know that the same applies to three? It is said: "In the midst of the judges he judges" (Ps. 82:1). [Note: The minimum number of judges in a court is three.] Whence do we know that the same applies even to two? It is said: "Then those who revered the Lord spoke to each

other, and the Lord listened and heard" (Malachi 3:16). [Note: "each other" assumes two speakers.] Whence do we know that the same applies even to one? It is said: "In every place where I have my name mentioned I will come to you and bless you" (Exod. 20:24). [Note: Here "you" can refer to even one individual.]

Furthermore, the Talmudic academy which is called ישיבה "Yeshiva" in Hebrew, is a place where the Divine Presence rests. This is evident from the letters of the word itself "יש ה'/ בה," "God is there." Thus we are assured that the Divine Presence is indeed present while our rabbis learn and make halachic decisions based on the Torah, all of which is done naturally לשם שמים, for the glory of God. And the Talmud Yerushalmi Sanhedrin 10:2 affirms, "If there are no prophets, there is no Divine Spirit, and if there is no Divine Spirit, there are no houses of worship and houses of study."

It should be emphasized that since the destruction of the Holy Temple and the absence of the Sanhedrin (The Great Assembly, where religious laws were interpreted and new enactments instituted), new rabbinic enactments have been made by only a select few, exceptionally distinguished, halachic authorities of each generation. The institution of new enactments demands a very extensive and deep knowledge of the Torah, the Talmud, and other sources of the Jewish law, as well as exceptional fear of God and dedication to the basic tenents of Judaism. It is a sad fact that the overwhelming majority of those bearing the title of "rabbi" today do not begin to meet these necessary standards and qualifications.

Though it may be true that economic, political, and social considerations of the times had an influence upon the shape of the new laws, such considerations were included if they were consistent with the teachings of the Torah. As such, the laws and regulations were formulated within a framework characterized by a high concern for social justice and morality.

The Talmud devotes much discussion to the laws governing the rights of daughters in the household of their parents and the rights of wives. For example, according to the Talmud, girls have complete freedom in choosing their husbands. Parents are not permitted to marry off a daughter before she attains maturity (defined by Jewish law as twelve years and one day) and then only after the daughter makes her own choice. If the parents do marry her off while she is a minor, when she reaches maturity she can repudiate the marriage and have it annuled without a divorce (Kiddushin 41a).

There are a number of Talmudic sayings that demonstrate the love and respect enjoyed by a Jewish wife. The following are a few examples: "An unwed man is no human being, because it is written, male and female He created them, He called them 'human beings'" (Yebamot 63a). Another sage said, "He who lives without a wife lives without joy, blessing, and goodness" (Yebamot 62b). Rabbi Josi used to say, "I used to say, 'I never called my wife "my wife," I always called her "my house," since it is said, "A man's wife is his house"'" (Sabbath 118b).

Jewish family life is generally known for its success and happiness. This is largely due to minute instructions on how to lead a married life given us by our sages of blessed memory. The rabbis were well aware of the physiology and psychology of human beings and the needs of the average man and woman.

Because they understood the ways of men, they also knew that life's ordinary stresses could easily cause people to forget and transgress the laws of the Torah. The following is a clear illustration. When Rabbi Ishmael heard of the enactment of the rabbis that one should not read by lamplight on the Sabbath, lest one inadvertently turn the wick up or down (and thus transgress a law of the Sabbath), he thought that the possibility of this happening was very remote. To prove this point, he personally set about reading by lamplight on the Sabbath . . . and did, in fact, forget himself and turned the wick. Rabbi Ishmael was then moved to admit that the sages were right (see Talmud Sabbath 12b).

The rabbis took everything into consideration in order to insure that Jewish marriages were happy, successful, and fulfilling. In so doing, they emphasized the wife's inalienable right to marital satisfaction. The following quotes by our sages illustrate the importance they attached to marital harmony. "What is a man to do to insure the well-being of his children? He must follow the commandment of Heaven and his wife." Another sage declared, "The husband must be considerate of his wife's honor, for all he has been blessed with is due to his wife" (Baba Metzia 59a).

The Talmud goes still further in emphasizing man's duty to be considerate of his wife. "If your wife is short, bend down to her" (Ibid). The husband is admonished, "Be careful not to bring your wife to tears, for God Himself will punish you for it" (Ibid). The husband is commanded "to love his wife like himself, but to put her honor above his." Although a man may not spend more than he can afford on his food and clothing, he is duty-bound to go above and beyond his means to please his wife. Rabbi Akiba said, "Who is rich? He who is blessed with a good wife" (Sabbath 25b).

In addition to the wealth of the Talmudic statements praising women or defining their status and obligations, there are a number of lines which emphasize other characteristics. Yes, it is true that the Talmud contains a number of "derogatory" remarks about women. However, it should be realized that these remarks are not meant to be taken literally. Unfortunately, at the present time, we do not know all the allegorical meanings of some of the puzzling remarks found in the Talmud. In answer to those who would accept these remarks in their literal sense, they should be advised that such statements do not have the force of law nor are they the authoritative substance of the Jewish weltanschauung. They are minority opinions and are neither normative nor authoritative.

A couple of lines about women are not the only "derogatory" phrases that should be taken in an allegorical sense. In order to illustrate the profundity and allegorical meaning of some Talmuldic statements in general, let us first consider the following puzzling remark from the Talmud Kiddushin 82a: טוב שברופאים לגהנם "The best of physicians go to hell." This enigmatic Talmudic statement is an explicit contradiction to the complimentary attitude of the sages towards medicine throughout the ages. Not only have Jewish scholars always shown great respect and esteem for the field of medicine, but many have also practiced medicine as a profession. Several editors of the Talmud, including Rabbi Chanina, Shmuel, Rabbi Ami, and Rabbi Yosi, were physicians. In later generations, many celebrated Jewish scholars practiced medicine; Rabbi Yehudah Halevi, Rambam and his son Rabbi Abraham, Ramban, and Seforno, among them.

Commenting on Exod. 21:19, our rabbis learn in the Talmud Berachot 60a that physicians are given biblical license to practice medicine. In fact, the field of medicine is accorded higher status than any other secular pursuit; Jewish law regards both the study and practice of medicine as a duty and religious obligation.

If all this is true, why does the Talmud condemn the best of the physicians to hell? Rashi understands this passage as referring to those physicians who do not care for patients in a diligent and appropriate fashion. A physician who might intentionally kill his patient or a physician who refuses to treat a poor patient who cannot afford his fees; these are the categories of physicians who go to hell. However, a more profound understanding of this statement can be attained through its allegorical meaning.

Every Hebrew letter has an assigned numerical value. The combined numerical value for the word טוב "tov" (in

English, "the best") is 17. There are 18 blessings in the daily prayer; one of these blessings acknowledge God as the Healer. Then, in an allegorical sense, a physician who prays only 17 blessings and leaves out the blessing acknowledging God as the Healer, the physician who is so arrogant that he forgets that he is merely God's emissary to help the sick, is the one who goes to hell.

Thus, the statement in the Talmud Kiddushin 82a is an attempt to warn the physician to be humble and constantly be aware that God is the ultimate healer.

The following statement from the Talmud Sabbath 152a seems very "derogatory": "Though a woman be as a pitcher full of filth and her mouth be full of blood, yet all speed after her." However, learning this quote in its proper context, that is, by understanding the theme immediately preceding this remark—namely God's decree that men shall desire women and go after them—we learn that the word "filth" is but an allegorical reference to the vaginal discharge and "mouth" refers to the vagina (see Maharsha). So the sentence can be translated to mean that even when a woman is menstruating and having vaginal discharge, men still desire her.

The opinion that women are lazy expressed in the Talmud Sanhedrin 7a as, "As she slumbers the basket falls," is countered by the opinion that "It is not a woman's way to sit at home idle," (Ketubot Yerushalmi 30a). The statement, "Whoever follows his wife's advice falls into hell," is deduced from the extreme instance of King Ahab who followed the advice of his wicked wife, Jezebel, obviously to his detriment. This simply means that not all wives, like not all husbands, are perfect. This idea is echoed in Erubin 41b, "Among those who will never behold the face of hell is he who has a bad wife," (the reason being, he has expurgated his sins in this world through exceptional suffering).

In a similar vein, one may better understand the statement made by King Solomon, "And I find the woman more bitter than death. . . ," (Ecclesiastes 7:26), after reading the rest of the verse where the particular object of Solomon's bitterness is revealed. That is, a woman ". . . whose heart is snares and nets, and whose hands are bonds . . ." (Ibid). A discussion in the Talmud Yebamot 63a sheds additional light upon Solomon's words. In discussing this verse, the Talmud tells of the behavior of Rab's wife. "Rab was constantly tormented by his wife. If he told her, 'Prepare me lentils,' she would prepare him small peas; (and if he asked for) small peas, she prepared him lentils."

The Talmud continues, "As soon as a man takes a wife his sins are buried; for it is said: 'Whoever finds a wife finds happiness and obtains favor of the Lord" (Proverbs 18:22). Commenting on this verse Raba states:

> Come and see how precious is a good wife and how baneful is a bad wife; for it is written: whoever finds a wife finds happiness." Now, if the Scripture speaks of the woman herself, then how precious is a good wife whom the Scripture praises. However, if the Scripture [allegorically] speaks of the Torah, then how precious is a good wife to whom the Torah is compared. 'How baneful is a bad wife,' for it is written, "And I find the woman more bitter than death." Now if the Scripture speaks of herself, then how baneful is a bad wife whom the Scripture censures. However, if the Scripture speaks of hell, then how baneful is a bad wife to whom hell is compared.

Taken in this context, one may understand why the sages made pronouncements such as, "Any evil, but not an evil wife" (Talmud Sabbath 11a). Or, "One ages faster because of an evil wife" (Midrash Tanchuma on Chayai Sarah 2).

A characteristic attributed to women by the Talmud is their partiality for the occult, a trait comfirmed by writers of other cultures. Therefore, we find in Yoma 83b, "Women are addicted to witchcraft." "The more women the more witchcraft" (Mishnah Abot 2:7). "The majority of women are inclined to witchcraft" (Sanhedrin 67a). And for that reason the biblical command, "Thou shall not suffer a witch to live" (Exod. 22:17), appears in the feminine gender.

The statement, "Most women are light-minded" (Kiddushin 80b, Sabbath 33b), as used in the context of the Talmud, never referred to the intellectual abilities or moral character of women. In this regard, Rashi on Avodah Zarah 18b relates what happened to Bruriah, the greatest female rabbinic scholar in Jewish history. As the story goes, one day Bruriah ridiculed the rabbinic dictum that women are "light-minded." Rabbi Meir, her husband, soon after asked one of his students to test her virtue. After repeated attempts, Bruriah finally succumbed to the student's advances. Thus, apparently Rashi's conclusion is that most women under intense pressure will yield more easily than most men. (Case in point, though Joseph, son of Jacob, was pressured, even threatened many times by Potifar's wife to have relations with her, he never yielded. See Talmud Yoma 35b).

Again the Talmud's statement is not an attack on the moral character of women. What is meant is that women are more easily beguiled, as Rashi learns in his commentary on Gen. 3:15. This statement also reflects a well known fact, namely that women are generally more sensitive and emotional than men—that women's minds generally have a greater sensitivity to intuitive and emotional values. And that is why we find in Megillah 14b, "Women are compassionate." And "Women are more compassionate than men" (Rashi on Kings II 22:14).

5
The Women of the Talmudic Era

Although women did not make original contributions to the Talmud, the Talmud does mention a few women who stood out for their exceptional character, perception, and intelligence.

Ima Shalom, an intellectually gifted woman, was the daughter of Rabbi Simon ben Gamliel, the president of the Sanhedrin in Jerusalem. She married Rabbi Eliezer ben Hyrkanus, an accomplished and outstanding scholar of his time. Ima Shalom's extraordinary intelligence and sense of humor is illustrated here.

A prominent gentile once mocked Rabbi Gamliel, Ima Shalom's brother, by saying, "Your God is a thief; for He stole a rib from Adam," (see Talmud Sanhedrin 39a). Ima Shalom asked her brother for permission to answer him. Then she said to the gentile, "Last night a robber broke into my house and carried away my silver vessels, leaving golden ones in their place." Thereupon the gentile said, "Would such robbers visit my house every night." Ima Shalom retorted, "This is exactly what happened to Adam. God took from him a rib and gave him a wife for it." The gentile then argued, "Still, God should not have put him to sleep, to take from him the rib by stealth." The clever Ima Shalom then ordered some raw meat to be brought, and she had it roasted before the gentile's eyes. Subsequently she invited him to partake of the meat. The gentile, however, turned away in disgust, recalling the undesirable sight of the blood dripping from the raw meat while the servants were preparing the roast. Ima Shalom turned to the gentile and said, "You see, Adam, too, would have felt disgust if he had witnessed how God formed woman from his rib; this is why He put him to sleep."

The following narrative further demonstrates Ima Shalom's superior insight and understanding. Ima Shalom's husband, Rabbi Eliezer, after disagreeing with several decisions made by the Sanhedrin, was finally excommunicated by order of his brother-in-law, Gamliel, the Sanhedrin's president. Consequently, the brothers-in-laws' relationship became rather strained. Ima Shalom, sure of her husband's innocence, feared that his penitential prayers might harm her brother Gamliel. She asked her husband to pledge that he would refrain from reciting these penitential prayers. However, on one occasion shortly thereafter, Rabbi Eliezer forgot his pledge and recited the penitential prayers. Ima Shalom overheard him and cried, "You have killed my brother!" Surprisingly, a short time later a messenger delivered news of Galmiel's death.

Another exceptional woman of the Talmudic era was Bruriah, the daughter of Rabbi Hanina ben Tradyon, and the wife of the famous Rabbi Meir. Rabbi Meir used to say that Bruriah always opened her mouth with wisdom. The Talmud Pesachim 62b credits Bruriah with studying three hundred legal decisions a day (even according to those who hold that the number 300 is a hyperbole commonly used in the Talmudic literature, it is still a testimony to the scholarship of Bruriah), and some of the rabbis even endorsed a decision of hers. Bruriah, like Ima Shalom, had a keen sense of humor. A story is told that a pious sage asked her in the street, "Which is the road to Lydda?" She answered him by asking how he could have forgotten the admonition of our sages, "Do not speak much to women." Then she told him that he could have phrased his question in just two words, "Where Lydda?"

On one occasion, Rabbi Meir, angry with his sinful neighbors, prayed to God that they be destroyed. He based his action on his understanding of the following Psalm (104:35), "Let 'chataim' (sins) cease out of the earth." Bruriah then explained to her husband that the Psalmist did not say 'chot'im' (sinners) but 'chataim' (sins) and that it is written at the end of the psalm, "and the wicked will be no more." All this means that sins and wickedness should be destroyed, not the sinner and the wicked, (see Talmud Berachot 10a). Rabbi Meir accepted Bruriah's interpretation and, in fact, it was adopted by many later Talmudic sages.

A convert to the Christian faith once mocked Prophet Isaiah's saying (54:1), "Sing O' barren, thou that did not bear...," asking why a childless woman should be happy because of her affliction. Bruriah explained to him that the answer to his question lies at the end of the passage, "For more are the children of the desolate than the children of the married wife, said the Lord." (Obviously, the gentile was unaware of the allegory implied by the verse. The "barren woman" is Jerusalem, the "children of the desolate" are children of Jerusalem, and the "married wife" are the nations of the world whose "husband," referring to their god, unlike Israel's God, has not deserted them. Therefore, the prophet is giving comfort to Israel by saying that even though the Temple is destroyed and Jerusalem is in ruin, in the future, when God redeems Israel from all her troubles, she will outnumber and be more powerful than the nations of the world, (see Talmud Berachot 10a).

It is both astonishing and admirable to see how well Bruriah coped with the tragic death of her two young sons, and how she managed to help her husband accept the reality with grace and a good heart. The tragedy occured on a Sabbath afternoon. Rabbi Meir was teaching at the house of study when the two boys died suddenly and unexpectedly. When Rabbi Meir returned home, Bruriah greeted him calmly. Rabbi Meir asked her, "Where are my sons?" She replied, "Most likely they are still at the house of study." The worried Rabbi Meir then said, "But I have not seen them there." Bruriah calmed him until after he had said the 'havdalah' (special prayers at the conclusion of the Sabbath). Then Bruriah told him, "Some time ago a friend entrusted to me some jewels for safe-keeping. Now he demands them back. Shall I return them to him?" Rabbi Meir replied, "Of course. I am astonished that you even ask this question." Bruriah then took her husband to the room where the bodies of their dead sons were lying. Rabbi Meir cried, "My sons! My sons!" Bruriah gently rebuked him, "Did you not say we must return to the owner the jewels he entrusted to us? The Lord gave, the Lord has taken away, blessed be the name of the Lord."

Rabbi Meir maintained a tolerant attitude toward women's education; his classes were open to the general public and women were freely admitted to them. One woman in particular, by the name of Hamta, regularly attended his lectures. It happened that one Friday evening before going to Rabbi Meir's lecture, Hamta forgot to fill the lamp in her house with oil. As a result, her house was dark when she returned home. Her enraged husband told her that she could not come into the house until she had spat at Rabbi Meir. When the wise and compassionate Rabbi Meir learned of the couple's dispute, he feigned an eye problem and asked the woman to spit seven times in his face to cure him of his affliction. (During that period, it was generally believed that spit was beneficial for eye ailments.) He then sent her back home and told her to tell her husband that she had complied with his request. When Rabbi Meir's disciples saw this, they were astonished that so great an authority on the Torah would let himself be so humiliated. But Rabbi Meir told them, "There is no sacrifice too great to reconcile a husband and a wife."

Rabbi Judah Hanasi's maidservant was considered another exemplary model of piety and moral character during the Talmudic era. Not much is known about this extraordinary woman who managed the household of the Mishnah's editor. The little that we do know comes from her salient remarks upon the interpretation of difficult biblical expressions. Once she saw a father beating his grown son in public. She angrily denounced him and pronounced the so-called "second degree excommunication" against him. Apparently, her understanding of the biblical injunction, "Thou shall not put a stumbling block before the blind" (Lev. 19:14), justified her actions: She reasoned that by punishing his adult son in public, the father would cause his son to sin against him by inciting the son to lift up his hand against his father, a mortal sin according to Jewish law.

The Talmud Ketubot 104a relates the following interesting narrative. Upon seeing Rabbi Judah on his death bed, struggling and suffering with pain (he was afflicted by what appears to have been an incurable and debilitating intestinal disorder), the faithful maidservant went up to the roof and prayed to the Lord that He put an end to her master's anguish. But her prayer could not be heard by God because Rabbi Judah's disciples had gathered in the courtyard to pray for his recovery. The clever maidservant took a vessel and threw it into the midst of the crowd. Distracted by the vessel, the disciples stopped praying for a moment, and in that moment Rabbi Judah's sufferings ended as his soul departed this world.

Rabbi Akiba is one of the most unique, creative, ingenious and extraordinary personalities in the Talmud. However, if not for his wife, he might never have attained such a high degree of scholarship, and the Jewish nation would have been deprived of a great sage.

Throughout Jewish history, education, knowledge, and scholarship have been highly valued. Our tradition teaches that it does not matter whether a man is wealthy, but it is very important that he strive to be highly knowledgeable and educated in the Torah. For thousands of years, the community of Torah scholars has been considered to be the Jewish aristocracy.

Akiba ben Joseph was originally known as an 'Am Ha-aretz,' an unlearned man. He was aware of his inferior social position and was greatly antagonistic toward Torah scholars. He was said to have once threatened, "If I could but lay hands on those proud learned men, I would bite them even quicker than a wild donkey."

Rachel was the name of the daughter of Kalba Sabua, one of the wealthiest citizens of Jerusalem. She was attracted to the young Akiba, who happened to be the shepherd of her father's flock. Rachel knew that Akiba was an 'Am Ha-aretz' but she also recognized his brilliant and creative mind. She consented to marry him on the condition that Akiba would cultivate his brilliance by studying at the Talmudic academies.

Kalba Sabua was displeased with his daughter's decision, to say the least. After she married Akiba, he banished her from his house and refused to support her in any manner at all. The married couple, too poor to maintain a permanent home, lived modestly by moving from one city to another. Rachel, ever the devoted wife, cut off her long, beautiful braids and sold them to help support her family while Akiba was busy learning at the Talmudic academies.

So passed several years. Rachel worked at home while her husband immersed himself in learning at the academies. Meanwhile, Rabbi Akiba became a celebrated scholar, well versed in the Torah and the Talmud. After being ordained as a rabbi and a teacher, he returned to Jerusalem accompanied by a large group of disciples. Rachel, who had long awaited her husband's return, rushed to greet him, falling at his feet. Immediately, one of the disciples pushed the poorly dressed woman aside. Akiba quickly told his disciple, "Don't! All I am, I owe to her, and you, too, must be grateful to her, for if it were not for her you could not have learned from me," (see Talmud Ketubot 62b, 63a). Thus, we see how this self-sacrificing and idealistic woman achieved greatness through her contribution to the accomplishment of others.

Rabbi Akiba always remembered his indebtedness to Rachel. He honored her to such an extent that the wife of the Nasi (the leader), Rabbi Gamliel II, complained to her husband that he did not honor her nor give her precious presents, as Akiba did to Rachel. Rabbi Gamliel's answer was, "Not every wife has done for her husband what Rachel did for Akiba." And so it was not surprising that Rabbi Akiba is quoted as saying, "A virtuous wife is the most precious treasure in the world." (See Talmud Sabbath 25b.)

As illustrated in the preceding section, the moral strength and courage of their women enabled the Jews of each generation to survive and overcome major crisises of their lives and times. Moreover, from earliest history, the special talent and gifts of women were recognized by Judaism, and Jewish women rose to positions of leadership in societies where women were generally powerless. They have always assumed a variety of roles. In fact, there hardly exists an area of human endeavor—be it domestic, economic, intellectual, political or religious—where Jewish women have not left an indelible mark.

Part Two
WOMEN AND SOME BASIC CONCEPTS IN JUDAISM

I
The Unified Role of Man and Woman

After a careful examination of the Jewish code of law and other sources of Jewish jurisprudence, it is not difficult to prove that men and women are of equal importance. In Genesis 1:27 we find: "And God created the man in His own image, in the image of God He created him, male and female He created them." This verse stands as a "Declaration of Equality" by God Himself.

The Talmud interprets the above verse as follows: God first created a self-sufficient androgynous being. But then He decided it was not good for the human being to be totally on his own, self-sufficient, and devoted only to himself. Therefore, He divided this self-sufficient being into two separate human beings—one male and one female. Each of these human beings was then given his/her own personality, talent, and role. With this division, God created two half organisms which were to be reunited through marriage. "Therefore shall a man leave his father and his mother and cleave unto his wife and they shall become as one flesh" (Gen. 2:24).

Since Adam was originally both male and female and was created in God's image, we may conclude that God himself is a combination of femininity and masculinity. And in fact, in the *Kedusha* (sanctification) prayer, God is addressed in both feminine and masculine terms. The world itself is said to have been created both as feminine and masculine—*shomayim,* heaven, is masculine; *eretz,* earth, is feminine.

The *Zohar* states that God does not cause His divine presence to dwell in a place where a male does not dwell with his female counterpart, nor are God's blessings found in such a place. Indeed, God did not bless Adam until his female counterpart was created (Zohar, Gen. 5:5). Thus, both God and His blessings are a combination of masculinity and femininity, and He planted this combination in the world which He created and in man, as well.

The masculine qualities of the male are distinctly different from, and often opposite to, the feminine qualities of the female. The male is distinguished for his aggressiveness, coldness, and objectivity. The female is considered more passive, emotional, intuitive, compassionate and merciful. All of these qualities are needed in order to maintain and continue God's creation. Both "justice" (masculine) and "mercy" (feminine) are divine. Together they are a blessing; one without the other would be considered a destructive curse.

The Creator is known by two names, Lord and God. Lord refers to the quality of justice, whereas God is His quality of mercy. It is written, "In the beginning the Lord (justice) created the heaven and earth" (Gen. 1:1). The Torah does not say that God (mercy) created heaven and earth and our Sages learn from this that the Almighty originally intended to create the world and guide it solely through the attribute of justice. But realizing that the world could not thus endure, He added His attribute of mercy. "In the day the Lord (justice) God (mercy) made earth and heaven" (Gen. 2:4). (Also see Rashi on Gen. 1:2.)

Similarly, the male without the female, and vice versa, would bring destruction to the world. The male's aggressiveness and calculation, if not combined with the female's qualities of passivity, emotionality, and compassion, can cause the destruction of humanity. Therefore, the question of whether man is superior to woman or vice versa is totally irrelevant. Either sex without the other is incomplete.

Completion and perfection only occur when men and women share their lives—when they function as one unit, with each half performing his or her own unique tasks.

The Raavad (Rabbi Abraham Eben Davud) apparently understands the true meaning of Gen. 1:27 wherefore man was created first, and then woman. His beautiful words extolling the unity of man and woman are reprinted below:

> It is for this reason that God saw fit to change the order of creation when He came to man, for had He created man and woman from the earth, each independently, each would have gone his own way. Husband and wife would not be designated one for the other to live together, for they would have been created separately. Rather God created woman from man so that they should live together as one unit each one needing the other.

So a man or a woman alone cannot fulfill God's mission; but they may do so together as one unit. They are like a single entity occupying two bodies. It is no wonder, then, that Jewish law dictates that a man must be as concerned about his wife as he would be about himself, since, in a real sense, wife and husband are part and parcel of one another. The Talmud Sanhedrin 28b and Rambam in Hilchot Edut 13:6 subscribe to this idea by declaring husband and wife are one. Likewise, one can deduce this idea of unity from the following biblical verse: ויאמר ה' אלהים לא טוב היות האדם לבדו אעשה לו עזר כנגדו "And God spoke, it is not good that man shall be alone, I shall make him a helpmate unto him" (Gen. 2:18).

Rabbi Samson Raphael Hirsch[1] ingeniously expounds on the above verse:

---
[1] *The Pentateuch,* Judaica Press, 1982, pp. 64–65.

Man was there, and all about him all the beauties of the Paradise blossomed, and still God did not pronounce His "Good!" It did not say: לא טוב לאדם היותו לבדו, that "It was not good for man to be alone" but, לא טוב היות אדם לבדו "This is not good; man being alone." As long as man stands alone it is altogether not yet good. The goal of perfection which the world is to attain through him will never be reached as long as he stands alone. The completion of "Good" was not man but woman, and it was only brought to mankind and the world by the woman.

Hirsch then adds that the above idea was deeply appreciated by the rabbis who taught in the Talmud:

Only through his wife does a man become a "man," only husband and wife together are "Adam." A task which is too great for one person must be divided, and just for the accomplishments of the whole of the man's mission, God created woman for man. And this woman is to be עזר כנגדו (helpmate). Even looked at quite superficially, this designation expresses the whole dignity of woman. It contains not the slightest reference to any sexual relationship. She is placed purely in the realm of man's work, it was there that she was missing, she is to be עזר כנגדו. And עזר כנגדו certainly expresses no idea of subordination, but rather complete equality and on a footing of equal independence. Woman stands to man כנגדו parallel, on one line, at his side.

The Midrash Genesis Rabbah teaches us, "God did not create woman from man's head, that he should not command her; nor from his feet, that she should not be his slave...; but rather from his side, that she should be near to his heart." Clearly, man and woman are equally important, and woman's creation *from man* by no means implies any inferiority on her part. In fact, it may even imply *superiority,* since woman was not created from the dust of the earth as were man and the animals, but rather from a body of a human being.

According to the *Kabbalah* (Jewish mystic literature), there are different categories (levels) of beings. The lowest level is inorganic matter, above it are the plants, still higher are the animals, and the highest is man. The ones at the lower level serve those at the higher levels, and man—who is at the highest level—serves the Lord who is above and beyond all that exists. So, too, in this sense, one might say woman is superior to man, because man was formed from the dust of the earth, whereas woman was formed from a human being who is at the highest level of the ontological hierarchy.

The idea of male and female unity is further reaffirmed every Sabbath day at *Kiddush* (blessing over the wine): "You shall not do any manner of work, you, and your son, and your daughter, your manservant, and your maidservant, and your cattle, and your stranger who is within your gates" (Exod. 20:9). There is no mention of "your wife" in this verse. Thus, it is obviously taken for granted that "you" and "your wife" are one. This same idea is echoed in Deuteronomy 12:18. When discussing the obligation of eating the tithe in the place selected by God, we again find no mention of the wife: "You and your son and your daughter and your manservant and your maidservant and the Levi who is within your gates. . . ."

In connection with the holiday of Succoth, a similar language is used. "And you shall rejoice before the Lord your God, you, and your son, and your daughter, and your manservant, and your maidservant, and the levite that is within your gates, and the stranger, and the orphan, and the widow that are in your midst . . ." (Deut. 16:11). Is it possible that the All-Merciful forgot the wife in this instance? The answer to this question is definitely in the negative. "You" refers to the husband and wife as one unit.

So we learn that all human beings are considered incomplete as long as they are not married. As Rabbi Elazar said in the Talmud Yebamot 63a: "An unwed man is no human being." And in Gen. 2:24 we find: "Therefore, a man shall leave his father and his mother and shall cleave to his wife, and they shall be one flesh." Furthermore, from Gen. 1:28

we can see that marriage and family are integral parts of the Divine Plan, as He commands the human race: "And God blessed them, and God said to them be fruitful and multiply and replenish the earth . . ." It is through marriage, that completion and unity is achieved.

As was previously noted, the physical creation of woman was a distinct phenomenon. She was created from the body of a man—unlike animals and unlike man who were created from the dust of the earth. Then the man called her his "Woman, because out of man was this (one) taken," (Gen. 2:23). Further on in Genesis (3:20) it says: "And the man called the name of his wife Eve, because she was the mother of all living things. Dr. Moshe Meiselman, in his book, *Jewish Woman in Jewish Law*[2] comments on this name assignment:

> That it is not an arbitrary title assignment but is also an essential part of role definition. To give Eve the name "mother of all life" is to assign her that task as her fundamental though not exclusive role. . . . Man's naming of woman is unlike his naming of animals. Whereas man's imposition of names upon the beasts asserts his cognitive superiority and physical mastery over them, in Eve's case his name acknowledges God's will acting independently of and prior to his own. The name Eve is given only after God has given a second role assignment in Genesis 3:16 as a result of the initial sin of Adam and Eve.

And on a deeper level, woman's creation *out of man* can be taken allegorically to mean that as long as man and woman are not joined into one, they remain incomplete.

---

[2] Ktav Publishing House, New York, 1978, p.11.

2
The Unique Character of Women

A tenet of Judaism, particularly pertinent to women, is the Jewish concept of modesty. As Dr. Meiselman[1] reflects:

> Modesty is the inner-directed aspect of striving, the essence of the Jewish heroic act. Woman was enjoined to develop this trait of personality to its highest degree. This is symbolized by the fact that woman was created from a part of the body which is private in two senses—first, it is generally clothed, and second, it is located beneath the skin.

It should be emphasized that in Judaism, "hidden from public view" does in no way imply inferiority. For example, when the angels came to visit Abraham, they asked him, "Where is Sarah your wife?" And Abraham replied, "Behold, in the tent" (Gen. 18:9). Rashi comments that, according to our sages, Sarah was a modest person. Only a few chapters later, we learn that Sarah attained a higher spiritual stature than her husband Abraham. As written in Genesis 21:12, we read that God instructs Abraham, "All that Sarah tells you, hearken to her voice." Again Rashi comments, "This teaches us that Sarah was superior to Abraham in prophecy." Thus, the fact that Abraham took a public role, does not—by any means—imply personal

---

[1] *Ibid.*, pp. 11, 12.

importance or spiritual greatness. The real hero here is Sarah—a hero of the inner, not outer stage.

The highly desirable trait of modesty is not restricted to women alone. Many of our greatest male spiritual leaders have been known for their modest behavior. Probably the best example lies with our teacher Moses who—as the only prophet who spoke to God on a one-to-one basis—achieved the highest degree of spirituality among all men. The Scriptures describe him thus: "... and the man Moses was exceedingly modest above all the men that [were] upon the face of the earth" (Num. 12:3).

Modesty has always been one of Judaism's most cherished traits. The Talmud has this to say about an immodest person: "He who walks in pride is as if he denies the existence of God" (Berachot 43b).

Now we can understand the meaning behind King David's words: כל כבדה בת מלך פנימה ממשבצת זהב לבושה "The entire glory of the daughter of the king lies on the inside surpassing the golden setting in her raiment" (Ps. 45:14). (There are several other translations for this verse, which will be cited later on.)

King David's words, which underline the Jewish attitude toward women in Jewish life, have been used by the sages in two ways. On the one hand, it has been cited throughout rabbinic literature as a description of the chastity and modesty of the Jewish woman, who is considered no less a princess than the king's daughter. On the other hand, it has been read as praise for the private nature of religious experience as a whole. The Midrash holds that true achievement is always attained in the private sphere, the one not visible to the public eye. From this verse, our sages learn that the glory of the Jewish wife and mother is to be found in the inner chambers of her own home, which is her palace and her royal domain. Rambam in Hilchot Ishut 13:11 writes:

> Every woman should go out to visit her parents or to console the mourners or to rejoice at weddings or to perform acts of

kindness for her friends, for a wife is not to be imprisoned in her home, as if it were a dungeon . . . But it is a disgrace for a woman always to go into public places and main streets and a husband should dissuade his wife from acting thus . . . For the essence of a wife's beauty is to be enthroned in the corner of her home as it says, "The entire glory of the king's daughter lies on the inside."

Here, the Rambam emphasizes the importance of modesty in women. It should be noted that he does not advocate the idea that women's functions are defined *only* within the realm of the home, but rather advises them to be modest and engage in acts of kindness.

King David's words are further explained by the rabbis as follows: The garment of the modest Jewish woman, who resembles a precious jewel, is carefully tailored and measured to properly cover her body. The valuable trait of modesty pertains not only to a woman's deeds, but also to her dress. The Talmud Yerushalmi, Yoma 1:4 cites the following narrative to illustrate this concept:

There was once a pious woman named Kimchit who had seven sons, each of whom served in the office of the High Priest. The Sages asked her, "By virtue of which good deeds did you merit such honor?" She answered: "Not even the walls of my home ever saw a hair of my head uncovered. Neither did they ever see as much as the hem of my undergarment." So the Sages recited this verse: "The entire glory of the king's daughter lies on the inside." They related it to Kimchit and said that because she acted with extraordinary modesty, she merited sons who were High Priests, whose garments were set with gold.

The Midrash Numbers Rabbah 1:3 discusses the importance of privacy and modesty in the following manner:

And God spoke to Moses in the wilderness of Sinai (Num. 1:1). Before the tent of Assembly was erected, He spoke to him from the bush . . . and afterwards in the land of Egypt . . . and afterwards in Midian . . . and afterwards at Sinai . . . but after the Tent was erected He said: How beautiful is privacy! As it says, "To walk privately with your God" (Micah 6:8), and therefore, He spoke with him in the Tent. And so too did David say: "The entire glory of the daughter of the king lies on the inside, more so than the one who is clothed in golden garments" (Ps. 45:14). The daughter of the king is Moses, who is the king of the Torah. The one who is clothed in gold is Aaron (this refers to the eight golden garments worn by the High Priest). Hence, it is said that a woman who is private in her life (and hence plays Moses' role by emphasizing private religious experience), even if she is an Israelite, is deserving to marry a priest and give birth to High Priests. This is what the Holy-One-Blessed-be-He said: "It is my glory to speak on the inside."

When one ponders upon the behavior of the great individuals whose activities and beliefs shaped our national character, one can't help but discover blatant examples of that special quality of modesty. Our forefathers worshiped God privately, without fanfare, and nary a thought about the public admiration that would accrue to them as holy men. Purity of deed and purity of purpose occur when one seeks to impress only the Creator. It happens when a man is not performing for the public, when he seeks no admiration and expects no credit.

It is in this context that we understand the wisdom behind the classic Jewish legend which states that only through the merit of thirty-six hidden saintly persons of each generation is the world maintained. This highest of achievements is attained by the hidden saintly person—an unknown whose lifelong toil is for God's approval alone.

Moses, who spoke to God in private, achieved a higher level of spirituality than did Aaron, the High Priest, who performed his Divine service in public. We may therefore conclude that public exposure is more of a hindrance than a help in achieving higher spiritual levels.

The lives of men and women are both private and public, with neither sex restricted to just one area. According to our tradition, however, the private sphere is considered to be the primary one in a Jewish woman's life. Whenever life necessitates that a woman be active in public (as will be discussed later on), she should retain her modesty. Moreover, man, whose primary sphere is public, is constantly reminded that the highest achievements and the highest spirituality are attained in private.

Although our tradition stresses that the role of women is in the private domain, it does not by any means imply that our rabbis thought of women as being less intelligent or less capable than men. Just the opposite. In Genesis Rabbah 18:1 Rabbi Yosi ben Zemra declares that women are *more* intelligent than men. And certainly in the eyes of the Holy-One-Blessed-be-He, men and women are considered equally important and equally necessary for carrying out God's mission on earth.

3
The Mission of Human Beings and the Infinite Wisdom of God

The Holy-One-Blessed-be-He has created everything for a purpose, though often this purpose is concealed from us. The author would like to suggest that each one of us has two main missions in this world. The first one is the "revealed mission," that is, to live a holy life in accordance with God's will and to ensure the continuation of such a life by procreation, and then by instructing and leading our children onto the right path. In this way, man will become the footstool, the support and resting place of the Divine Presence, through fulfillment of this revealed mission.

Evidence for this mission lies in the following statements: "And now Israel, what does the Lord your God require of you, but to fear the Lord your God and to walk in all His ways, and to love Him, and to serve the Lord your God with all your heart and with all your soul. To keep the commandments of the Lord and His statutes which I [Moses] command you this day, for your good" (Deut. 10:12–13). The commandment regarding procreation is found in Genesis 1:28: "And God said to them [Adam and Eve], be fruitful and multiply and replenish the earth."

And, in fact, the Talmud Gittin 41b quotes the following verse from Isaiah 45:18: "For thus said the Lord that created the heavens, He is God that formed the earth and made it, He established it, He created it not a waste, he formed it to be inhabited . . ." The Talmud's comment on the last part of this verse is that the purpose of creation, as far as man is concerned, is not to make earth a waste land, but to inhabit it. Inhabitation of the earth can clearly be realized through procreation.

The final part of the "revealed mission" concerns instructing our children in the path of God. This we learn from the portion of Shema that states, "And you shall teach them [the commandments] to your children" (Deut. 6:7).

Our second mission remains unrevealed. Nevertheless, it is a major mission—one unique to each and every one of us, a mission that possibly incorporates myriads of smaller goals. It is the mysterious nature of this personal mission that makes life interesting and challenging.

In rare cases, one may claim with some confidence that this second mission has been such and such for so and so. For example, one may very well say that the major mission of Moses in this world was to lead the children of Israel out of Egypt and to later give them the Torah. Or that King David's mission was to unify the loosely federated tribes into a single nation and to further complete the conquest of the Promised Land. And it may be claimed that King Solomon's mission was to build the Holy Temple in Jerusalem.

However, due to our finite understanding and knowledge, we can never fully delve into God's infinite wisdom and purpose in creating us and in creating everything else around us. This may well be illustrated by the following Midrashic parable about David as a young man, before he was king:

> David sat in his garden and watched a flea attacking a spider. A madman came and chased both insects away with a stick. Then David said to the Holy-One-Blessed-be-He: "All that You created is beautiful, and wisdom is the most beautiful of all, however, of what value are these three creatures? The flea only bites, but contributes nothing. The spider weaves and weaves all year, yet no one can wear its web. What satisfaction can you derive from a madman walking about, ripping his clothing,

chased by little children, and mocked by all, and he has no concept of Your Greatness?"

God answered, "David, the time will come when you will need all three, and then you will recognize their purpose."

Later on, when David was fleeing from the wrath of King Saul, he hid in a cave. God in His mercy quickly sent a spider to spin a huge web across the cave's entrance. When Saul arrived at the cave, he saw the unbroken web, and assumed no one could have entered the cave without breaking the web. Saul then took a rest, giving David the opportunity to flee undetected. When David later discovered the spider, he exclaimed: "Blessed is your Creator who fashioned such wondrous creatures for this world."

Another time, David and his companion, Avishai, secretly entered Saul's camp and saw the mighty Abner, Saul's commander-in-chief of the army, sleeping next to Saul's head. Abner's legs surrounded Saul protectively, but his knees were raised. David slipped beneath Abner's knees and grabbed Saul's spear and jug. Suddenly, the sleeping Abner stretched out his legs, pinning David beneath them. David, unable to move for fear of waking Abner, silently pleaded to God for mercy. God accepted David's plea and sent a flea to bite Abner on the leg. When the flee bit, Abner drew up his knees, once again allowing David to escape unharmed.

Yet one more time, David escaped the wrath of Saul by fleeing to the land of the Philistines. David brought with him nothing but Goliath's sword, which he had taken after slaying the giant. It happened that Goliath's brothers served as bodyguards for Achish, king of the Palestinian city, Gath. They instantly recognized David because of Goliath's sword and asked the king to kill him and thus avenge their brother's death.

David was aware of the severity of his situation and, once again, entreated God to save him. He asked for a measure of madness—that same state he had once criticized. Then

David, feigning the ways of a madman, wrote on the city gates, "King Achish owes me one hundred myriads [coins] and his wife owes me fifty myriads." At the same time, God caused the wife and daughter of Achish to go mad as well. Thus the women screamed and raved insanely inside the palace while David raved outside the palace gates. Achish became irritated, and finally drove David away, saying to Goliath's brothers, "Am I lacking in mad people that you bring this fellow to rave in my presence?" (I Samuel 21:16). Once again David was saved.

So we see how David's life was saved by the very creatures he had thought to be purposeless and/or harmful. As a result of these vivid lessons, David perceived, as never before, the greatness of God's creation and His infinite wisdom.

For purposes unknown to us, the Holy-One-Blessed-be-He created man and woman and gave them dominion over His world: "And God blessed them and said to them, be fruitful and multiply, and replenish the earth and subdue it and have dominion over the fish of the sea and over the fowl of the heaven, and over every living thing that creeps upon the earth" (Gen. 1:28).

In order for the earth to be sustained and managed effectively under the dominion of human beings, the Lord assumed that a division of roles for man and woman was necessary. Just as a factory is most productive when each employee has an assigned task, so too, in the big factory of earth, is it essential to have assigned roles and responsibilities. It is evident that the Creator knows us even better than we know ourselves, and He is certainly well aware of our physical and psychological needs. Therefore, He is the only One who is able to tell us how to best serve Him and dominate His world.

God assigned roles to men and women in accordance with His good and benevolent judgement. This role assignment is clearly delineated in the Torah.

For man:

"By the sweat of your brow shall you eat bread until your return unto the ground, for out of it you were taken, for you are dust, and unto dust you shall return" (Gen. 3:19). Clearly man's primary role is to be the breadwinner, which is a public role. This function of man in God's world can also be inferred from the following: When Adam was expelled from the Garden of Eden, the Torah states: "And God sent him out of the Garden of Eden to work the earth from whence he was taken" (Gen. 3:23).

For woman:

אל האשה אמר הרבה ארבה עצבונך והרנך בעצב תלדי בנים ואל אישך תשוקתך והוא ימשל בך "Unto the woman He said: I will greatly multiply your pain and your travail, in pain you shall bring forth children and unto your husband [shall be] your desire and he shall rule over you" (Gen. 3:16). Here the implication is that woman's primary role is that of a mother and a wife. (The last part of this verse will be dealt with in detail further on.)

The concept of role assignment is found in other areas of Jewish life, as well. From among the tribes of the children of Israel, the tribe of Levi is singled out for specific service to God. And from among the tribe of Levi, the Holy-One-Blessed-be-He chose Aaron and his sons to do His holy service in the tent of meeting, in the tabernacle, and later on, in the Temple. God, in His infinite wisdom, saw these priests as fit to do His service and to bring the sacrifices of the children of Israel as atonement for their sins. Similarly, Moses' children and a number of other families within the tribe of Levi were assigned to be singers and perform other related services in the Holy Temple.

The tribe of Judah was chosen to rule over God's people, the children of Israel. As King David relates: "He chose the tribe of Judah, Mount Zion which He loves" (Ps. 78:68). "He chose David His servant, and He took him from sheep corrals. From behind the nursing ewes, He brought him to tend Jacob, His nation, and Israel, His estate" (Ps. 78:70-71). In II Samuel 22:51, in Psalms 18:51, and at the conclusion of the grace after meals, we find that God assigns kingship to David and his house forever. "He gives great salvation to His King and He performs kindness to His anointed; to David and to his seed, forever."

Finally, the Holy-One-Blessed-be-He chose the children of Israel to serve as an example to the nations of the world, and to exalt Him and to establish His Kingdom of Justice and Peace on earth. As the Scripture informs us: "For you are a holy people unto the Lord your God, and the Lord has chosen you to be a people of select portion unto Himself out of all the peoples that are upon the face of the earth" (Deut. 7:6). And in Zechariah 14:9 and at the conclusion of our daily prayers we recount, "And it is said: The Lord shall be King over all the earth; and on that day the Lord shall be One, and His name One." Likewise, we recite at the beginning of Pirkei Abot (The Ethics of the Fathers) and in the Talmud Sanhedrin 90a: "Every Jew has a portion in the World to Come." This line can be interpreted to mean that every Jew has a portion in the major mission that is entrusted to us—namely bringing about the establishment of the Lord's Kingdom.

All these choices and assignments were made by God in accordance with His good judgement, His infinite wisdom, and His understanding. Similarly, assigning woman's primary role in life to be that of wife and mother is also determined by God's infinite wisdom and understanding. We can rest assured that the Holy-One-Blessed-be-He had our best interests in mind when He assigned these various roles to us. We are told: "For you are children of the Lord" (Deut. 14:1). Is it not obvious that parents want the best for their beloved children? So too, the Holy-One-Blessed-be-He, our Parent in Heaven, who created us through His omniscience and benevolence, recognized what was best for us and assigned us roles for our own good.

Rabbi Samson Raphael Hirsch[1] derives the "whole task of the human race" from the verse "Be fruitful and multiply and fill the earth and subdue it" (Gen. 1:28). He says:

> פרו ורבו ומלאו ... וכבש. In these four words the whole task of the human race is expressed. In them are indicated marriage, the family, the state, and property, with moral foundation and significance of each. פרו [Ed. note: "be fruitful"] points out to marriage, the union of sexes for the production of new human beings. These created, בדמותם כצלמם, in spiritual and physical resemblance to their parents, are to carry in themselves all that is noblest and best both of divine and human that is inherent in the parents. The determined male element of the father and the receptive element of the mother unite in the child to produce a new personality, and form the inexhaustible variety of human character.
>
> רבו [Ed. note: "multiply"] points to the family. Nurse and fashion the offspring you have produced in your own likeness, so that you may reproduce yourselves through them. Without care and training the offspring becomes spoilt and wild ... The birth must so to speak be continued, the father and the mother must further unite their labors to tend, train and fashion the child, and this is practically nothing else than the continued transmission of what is best and noblest both of Divine and human in the parents to the children, in order that they may grow up in their image both spiritually and physically and that the parents may reproduce themselves in the children. The depth of thought embodied in the Hebrew vocabulary appears in the fact that רבו signifies both to increase and to train and bring up. Successful training is also the fruit of the united female and male forces in the parents ... The nursery of human culture is the house, the family, and it is when רבו makes

---

[1] Dayan Dr. I. Grunfeld, *Judaism Eternal* (Soncino Press, London, Vol. 2, 1956), pp. 52–53.

this goal of פרו that marriage, the union of sexes, acquires its ethical significance, its divine nobility, its world-building function.

מלאו [Ed. note "fill"] points to society, to the state. Since every married pair is told to "fill the earth," to see that the earth becomes and remains full of its noblest content, a mass of human beings, מלאו transcends the narrow circle of individual household, it calls upon everyone to help to establish and maintain as many families as possible on the earth, and makes all responsible for the existence and growth of all . . .

It is obvious that human beings are created for purposes that are known only to the Creator. However, each one of us is assigned our own particular role and function in this world, and the apparent purpose of this division of roles and functions is to enable us to live successful and fruitful lives, and to better serve our Creator and further His Divine Plan.

4
The Fulfillment of Women in Life

Most women consider having and raising children to be one of their major fulfillments in life. Yet, it appears from the commandment of procreation that women are not obligated to have children to the same extent as men. The reason for this could be that since it is so much a part of woman's nature to want children, there was no need to specifically command them in this regard. Having children has always been of ultimate importance, particularly to Jewish women. Children are a source of strength to the Jewish mother, as the Psalmist said: "Out of the mouths of babes and sucklings You have established strength" (Ps. 8:3).

Let us review some biblical evidence of a woman's desire for children. There is a well known dictum, "The deeds of the forefathers [the patriarchs] is a sign to the children [the Jewish people]" (see Sotah 34a). This saying surely applies to the deeds of the matriarchs as well. Sarah is the first woman we encounter in the Torah who expresses her deep aspiration to have a child. The Holy-One-Blessed-be-He realizes her life's goal, as we read on the first day of every New Year, "And the Lord remembered Sarah...," on which Rashi comments, "He remembered her with conceiving."

Rebecca is another example of a matriarch who was anxious to have a child, and asked her husband Isaac to join with her in praying to the Lord for conception (Gen. 25).

Leah, one of Jacob's wives, cherished the idea of having children to such an extent that even after four births, she still prayed to the Lord to give her more, and her prayer was answered (Gen. 30:17). Rashi comments that she was answered because she desired to increase the tribes. This implies that Leah's prayers were not due to jealousy of her sister or any other ulterior motive(s), but rather the result of a pure and natural desire that most women possess.

Rachel, Leah's sister and another of Jacob's wives, also put having children above everything else. The Torah testifies to the fact that Jacob loved Rachel more than he loved Leah; Jacob spent fourteen torturous years working for Laban (Leah's and Rachel's father) in order to win Rachel as his wife. Still, we find that Rachel was dissatisfied, and did not feel she has fulfilled her life's goal, until God answered her prayers and granted her children.

The book of Samuel begins with the story of Elkanah and his two wives, Channah and Peninnah. Elkanah used to go to Shiloh to offer sacrifices to God. He would give portions of the peace offerings to Peninnah and to all her sons and daughters. To Channah, who was childless, ". . . he would give one choice portion, for he loved Channah" (I Samuel 1:5). But Channah was sad, and she would weep and not eat her portion. Elkanah tried to comfort her: "Am I not better to you than ten sons?" (I Samuel 1:8) he'd say. But Channah would not be comforted because she was missing something very important—children. She entreated the Lord to give her a son, and she vowed a vow to God, ". . . and I shall give him to the Lord all the days of his life" (I Samuel 1:11). As we know, her prayers were answered and she later gave birth to Samuel who, in his generation, was equal to Moses, in his generation. Incidentally, this narrative is the *Haftorah* (the portion from the book of the prophets) that we read on the first day of the New Year. It is not surprising that on this day—when we are judged before the Holy-One-Blessed-be-He and our destiny for the coming year determined—we are twice reminded of the importance of having children, the central role women play in having children, and the significance of family life.

Rabbi Samson Raphael Hirsch, commenting on verse 16 in Genesis chapter 3 says, ". . . there is no higher happiness for a woman than to have children . . ."

King Solomon ends his book of Proverbs (31:10–31) by praising the אשת חיל ("woman of *chayil*"). The word חיל *chayil,* as used in the Bible, has various connotations; i.e.: wealth, skill, military force, general, competence, devoutness, valor, virtuous. In essence, it implies the presence of whatever skills or attributes are necessary to carry out the specified task(s).

In this hymn, King Solomon portrays the ideal image of a virtuous Jewish woman—a woman greatly immersed in the affairs of her household and in her roles as mother and wife. However, various biblical commentators assert that the hymn is allegorical. They have variously interpreted it as a reference to the Sabbath, the Torah, the Divine Presence, wisdom, and the soul. In any event, the very fact that the Jewish woman was chosen as the symbol for such an exalted spiritual display is, in itself, a magnificent tribute to her.

This famous song, אשת חיל, "Woman of Valor," or "Virtuous Woman," is sung by a husband to his wife every Friday night before officially starting the first festive meal of the Sabbath. The song is so beautiful, I've included it here, in English, in its entirety.

> Who can find a virtuous woman?
> For above pearls is her value.
> The heart of her husband doth safely trust in her,
> And he will not see his gain diminish.
> She treateth him well and not ill,
> All the days of her life,
> She seeketh wool and flax,
> She worketh willingly with her hands.
> She is like the merchant-ships;
> She bringeth her food from afar.

Some Basic Concepts

She riseth while it is still night,
And giveth food to her household,
And a portion to her maidens.
She thinketh of a field and buyeth it,
With the fruit of her hands she planteth a vineyard.
She girdeth her loin with strength,
And maketh strong her arms.
She perceiveth that her merchandise is good;
Her lamp goeth not out by night.
She layeth her hand to distaff.
And her hands hold the spindle.
She stretcheth out her hand to the poor;
Yea, she reacheth her hands to the needy.
She is not afraid of snow for her household;
For her household is clothed with scarlet.
She maketh for herself coverlets;
Her clothing is fine linen and purple.
Her husband is known in the gates,
When he siteth among the elders of the land.
She maketh linen garments and selleth them;
She delivereth girdles unto the merchants.
Strength and dignity are her clothing;
And she laugheth at the time to come.
She openeth her mouth with wisdom;
And the law of kindness is on her tongue.
She looketh well to the ways of her household.
And eateth not the bread of idleness.
Her children rise up, and call her blessed;
Her husband also, and he praiseth her;
"Many daughters have done valiantly,
But thou excelleth them all."
Grace is deceitful, and beauty is vain;
But a woman that feareth the Lord,
she shall be praised.
Give her of the fruits of her hands;
And let her works praise her in the gates.

In sum, the above poem eloquently conveys the traditional duties and privileges of the Jewish woman by describing an ideal model of the fulfilled wife and mother.

5
The Status of the Jewish Woman

It often seems that a person who achieves higher levels of spirituality is also burdened with greater restrictions and limitations. The fact that those close to God are judged most critically—to a hair—is a known principle in Judaism. For example, the *Kohanim,* the priests, who were designated by the Holy-One-Blessed-be-He to perform His service are restricted in various ways. They are commanded to stay away from all uncleanliness, and not to defile themselves by coming into contact with a dead body. The high priest, who attained the highest level of spirituality and was in the service of the Lord, was even exempted from going to his parents' funeral. Among all the tribes of Israel who received a portion in the land of Israel, only the tribe of Levi—consisting of the priests and the levites—did not receive any portion in the Promised Land.

Likewise, women, who are at a higher spiritual level than men as evidenced earlier (i.e. man was created from the dust of the earth, whereas woman was made from man—a higher level of being; and examples derived from various superior women throughout biblical times and from the generation of the exodus in particular) . . . because of this higher level of spirituality, women are restricted and limited in certain areas.

Furthermore, it is human nature to wish to protect the things that are very precious to us. For example, if one is trusted with an expensive, beautiful, and highly valuable piece of jewelry, one handles it with care, guards it in a safe place and only wears it on special occasions. So too, a woman, who is compared to "the invaluable pearl" and "the crown of her husband" by King Solomon, is to be protected from any defilement or devaluation. A woman's value lies in her modesty as it is written, "The entire glory of the daughter of the king lies within," and that is why the private role of women in Jewish life is so greatly emphasized.

Of course, limitations and restrictions carry with them privileges and benefits. According to our rabbis, one who loves his wife like himself and honors her more than he honors himself, is blessed with, "And you shall know that peace is your house," (Yebamot 62b). Rabbi Helbo said that a man should always be mindful of his wife's honor because blessing is found in his house only because of her as it is written: ". . . and it went well with Abraham because of her" (Gen. 12:16). Along these lines Rava told his townfolk, "Honor your wife so that you may become rich" (Baba Metzia 59a).

One rabbi said, "If your wife is short bend down and consult with her" (Baba Metzia 59a). Another rabbi explained that he never called his wife "my wife" but rather "my home" because all my needs are realized through her and she is the home in principle" (Gittin 52a). It is further written, "For a man who loses his first wife through death, it is as though he had witnessed the destruction of the Holy Temple, the world becomes dark for him, his steps become smaller, his designs are frustrated" (Sanhedrin 22a). And, "He who is without a wife is without help, without atonement, without life" (Genesis Rabbah 16). "But he who is of merry heart has a continual feast" (Proverbs 15:15), refers to a man who has a good wife (Baba Bathra 145b).

Rabbi Uriah taught that a man should drink less than what he has, and should clothe himself with what he has, but should honor his wife and children with more than he possesses. "If a man goads his wife to insult him by refusing her ornaments and finery, he becomes poor" (Sabbath 62b). Rav said that a man should be careful not to cause pain to his wife, to make her weep. Rabbi Elazar explained that ever since the Holy Temple was destroyed, the gates of prayer were closed to everything except weeping (Baba Metzia 59a). As it is written, "Hear my prayer, O' Lord, to my outcry, lend an ear, to my tears be not mute" (Ps. 39:13).

Rabbi Yosi said that when a woman is private within her house, she is worthy of marrying the high priest and begetting children who shall become high priests. Rabbi Pinhas the Kohen, the son of Hama, taught that when a woman is private within her house, just as the altar makes atonement for sins, so she atones for her household (Midrash Tanhuma 6).

It is written ויבן ה' אלהים את הצלע "And the Lord God built the rib" (Gen. 2:22). Rabbi Hisda explains that the word ויבן (built) comes from the same root as בינה, understanding. This teaches us that when the Holy-One-Blessed-be-He built woman from man's rib, He gave her more intelligence (Niddah 45b). If women are advised to avoid being out too much in public, it is because of the fear of *men's* misbehavior, not women's (see Gen. Rabbah, 8).

Finally, in the words of Rabbi Samson Raphael Hirsch:[1]

> While fully appreciating the special and deeply implanted characteristics of the female sex, the Sages attribute to it complete spiritual and intellectual equality with the male. In the very words with which the formation of man by the hands of God is proclaimed, וייצר ה' אלהים את האדם, they find an indication that the formation of both male and female is on the same

---

[1] Dayan Dr. I Grunfeld, *Judaism Eternal* (Soncino press, 1956), Vol. 2, pp. 95–96.

footing, יצירה לאדם יצירה לחוה (Gen. Rabbah 14). It is true that the Sages have a number of sayings pointing to the peculiar features of the feminine nature, especially its greater emotional susceptibility, such as: the man is easier to appease, the woman flares up more quickly, woman is more frequently stirred to tears (Gen. Rabbah 16, Sotah 17a, Baba Metzia 59a), and their deep remark that women have only one heart, their interest is less divided, always turned only to one object at a time (Yelamdenu); but at the same time they assign to a woman a greater intellectual endowment. Thus they say: The Creator has endowed the woman with a better mind than the man, therefore, the female sex reaches intellectual maturity earlier than the male (Niddah 45b). Hence, for the Sages of the Jewish people, its matriarchs, a Sarah, a Rebecca, are filled with the spirit of God and see with the spirit of God just as much as the patriarchs (Sanhedrin 69a, B.R. 67). Like the men, so the women are through the deliverance and election of Israel called to the highest spiritual and moral elevation of which mankind is capable (Sifra on Leviticus 26:13) . . . And the Sages mention with gratitude the spiritual lessons with which women have enriched the Jewish consciousness. From Leah we have learned to thank God, from Tamar to cast ourselves into the burning furnace rather than put a man to shame in public, from Channah, we have learnt to pray and recognize God as צבאות ה' (Berachoth 7, 31; Baba Metzia 58a). And in general, in the view of the Sages, every human being, no matter of what position, sex, race, or people, is capable of the highest spiritual and moral perfection.

We have seen that a wife, in Jewish law, receives a tremendous amount of honor and respect. She is, however, obligated to reciprocate for some of these privileges in a manner prescribed by the law. The following sayings illustrate this point.

Rama, in the name of Tanna de be Eliyahu said that a woman shall do her husband's will. Even though woman is man's partner, she should think highly of her husband, and then he will love her; and if she only speaks when necessary, she will be even more beloved by her husband; and if she talks to him with grace and with humility, then she will be exalted before him, exceedingly.

It is said in the Midrash that a wise woman told her daughter as she was getting married, stand before your husband as you might stand before a king, and if you treat him like you were his maid, he will be your bondman and will honor you like his master (*Menorat Hamaor Ner* 3, Rule 6, part 4, Ch. 2).

A man once told his wife to break an object upon Baba's head. (Baba the son of Buta was one of the greatest Sages of the time.) The woman found Baba sitting in the gate of the city and she went ahead and broke the object on his head. Baba asked her, "What did you do?" She replied, "Thus commanded my husband." He said to her, "You did your husband's will, may the Lord bless you with two sons like Baba ben Buta" (Nedarim 66b).

Rabbi Akiba taught that if a man and woman are deserving, the *Shechina*, the Divine Presence, will rest among them; otherwise, fire devours them (Sotah 17a). Rabbi Yehoshua ben Karha said that because man was made of flesh and blood, he was called "Adam" ("dam" in Hebrew means "blood"); after God made him a helper he was called איש (man), and his helper was called אשה (woman). What did the Holy-One-Blessed-be-He do? He put His name between them—the letters 'י' and 'ה,' God's "name" here symbolizes the Divine Presence. Thus we learn, if a husband and wife walk in His path and keep His commandments, the Divine Presence will be with them and they will be saved from all sorrows and afflictions. However, if they do not follow God, He will remove the letter 'י' from איש (man), and the letter 'ה' from אשה (woman), and they will become אש ואש, fire and fire. And fire eats up fire, as it says in Job 31:12, כי אש היא עד אבדון תאכל, "For it would be a fire that consumeth down (*Pirkei D'Rebee Eliezer*, ch. 13).

The above comes to teach us that there exists a consuming fire in the heart of every man and woman. When a man and woman marry, they bring two fires together that, if not properly tended, are capable of destroying the world. To extinguish the fire would be incompatible with life, for fire generates life in the world. However, it is impossible to leave the fire as it is because it generates evil as well. So what did the Holy-One-Blessed-be-He do? He placed one of the letters from His name, *Yud,* between *Aleph* and *Shin,* to make the name איש (man). And He placed the letter *Heh* after *Aleph* and *Shin* to make אשה (woman). Thus while both man and woman retain in their names the word אש (fire), when they are married in harmony and in accordance with God's will, the fire does not consume but rather gives warmth.

Since it is possible for the Divine Presence to exist among us if we deserve it, one may say that every Jewish home has the status of מקדש מעט (a miniature sanctuary). Those who dwell in it are like priests, and any function that takes place in there is like a sacred alter service. Even the wicked Balaam testified to this when he said: "How goodly are your tents, O' Jacob, your dwellings O' Israel" (Num. 24:5). Furthermore, God commanded us: "And let them make me a sanctuary that I may dwell among them" (Exod. 25:8). Thus the children of Israel made dwelling places for God wherever they wandered so that His Divine Presence would rest among them: in the wilderness, in Gilgal, in Shiloh, in Nob, in Gibeon, and in Jerusalem. As He promised, "Wherever I cause My Name to be mentioned I will come to you and bless you" (Exod. 20:24).

Now that all these dwelling places lie in ruin, along with our Holy Temple in Jerusalem, we are left with only one dwelling place of God that can never be destroyed, and that is the Jewish home. There the Divine Presence is served continuously, and eventually the Jewish home and the Jewish family will serve as a source of redemption for all Israel and all the world. How do we know this? The verse in Exodus 25:8 first speaks of a single sanctuary and then adds, "... and I will dwell among them" in the plural form. Clearly each Jewish home, i.e. each Jewish family, represents a sanctuary where God dwells.

The relationship between a husband and wife is like a two-way street. According to Jewish law, a husband is obligated to have relations with his wife on a regular basis. Rambam, in Hilchot Ishut 15:17–18, explains the husband's obligations thus: "He may not have relations with her against her will, but with her will and out of talking and happiness ..." Similarly, the sages commanded the woman not withhold herself from her husband in order to hurt him or to increase his love for her, but to listen to him whenever he desires her.

Our Sages commanded the husband to honor his wife more than he honors himself and love her as he loves himself. If he is wealthy, he should spend for her as much as and even more than his means permit. He should not make her fearful of him, but should talk to her softly. He should not be sad, nor quarrelsome. So, too, our Sages commanded the woman to honor her husband more than usual and to be modest. A Jewish woman is expected to be like the אשת חיל, the woman of valor, described by King Solomon. She is to occupy herself with doing good deeds, praying, studying, and creating a Jewish home.

As noted in the Introduction, because we live in a secular culture (like the United States), we can easily be influenced, misled, and misdirected by the values of that culture. Assimilation has been a highly destructive factor in the survival of the Jews and Judaism throughout our history. The key to Jewish survival lies in keeping the laws of our Torah, which is our ultimate value system. Thus we are commanded, "My ordinances you shall do, and My statutes you shall keep" (Lev. 18:4).

One example of a secular influence which is not wholly compatible with traditional Jewish ideals is the contemporary woman's desire to pursue a career and achieve financial independence. Years before anyone else was concerned with women's rights, a number of Jewish laws were enacted to protect a woman from being abused because of her lack of financial independence, and to assure that she be treated fairly. The Talmudic pronouncement, "A man should spend more money on his wife's needs than on his own" (Yebamot 62b), underlines the philosophy behind such laws.

Jewish law also provides the legal structures under which a woman is allowed to work and be financially independent. These laws were designed to help those women whose husbands, for one reason or another, do not or are unable to properly support their wives. However, the pursuit of financial independence by the wife has never been considered a primary goal, but rather a pursuit of last resort. Our Jewish tradition emphasizes that the *family* is the basic unit of Jewish life; and meant to function in a unified manner. When they marry, both men and women surrender their identities as independent individuals and become interdependent or, better yet, a single functioning unit. Separately, a man and a woman are incomplete, together they form a complete whole. As we learn from Genesis 2:24, "And they shall be one flesh." And therein lies the Jewish ideal, both financially and emotionally.

An exclusive secular life is an empty life. It is a futility; as King Solomon emphatically declared, "Futility of futilities—said Kohelet—futility of futilities! All is futile" (Ecclesiastes 1:2). King Solomon possessed everything a man could desire—huge homes, great wealth, entertainment, respect, and the obeisance of rulers (there is an opinion that Solomon ruled over the entire world—Sanhedrin 20b). Yet he, Solomon, the wisest of all men on earth, came to announce at the end of his life that all earthly strivings are inconsequential—futile and fruitless, as nothing remains of man's labor after his death. The Talmud notes that when a baby is born, his fist is closed, as if to say, "I am going to conquer the world and possess it." However, when a man dies, his hand is open, as if to say, "See, I did not take anything with me from this world" (Midrash Kohelet Rabbah 5:14).

Only those actions motivated by Torah ideals shall bring forth fruit, success, and eternity. It is very appropriate that we read the entire book of the Ecclesiastes (Kohelet) on the intermediate Sabbath of Succoth (the Feast of the Tabernacle). In celebration of this holiday, the Torah instructs us to leave our homes and dwell in makeshift booths. The *Succah* (booth) is to serve as a reminder of the emptiness and futility inherent in materialistic life. We must remember that eternity belongs to God and our strivings and preoccupations with worldy affairs are nothing but "the futility of futilities." However, all is not waste and futility. On the last day of the Feast of the Tabernacle, we celebrate the holiday of *Simchat Torah* (rejoicing of the Torah). And it is on that day, that we are truly happy, as the Torah says, והיית אך שמח "And you shall be altogether joyful" (Deut. 16:15). The *real* joy, the real eternity, and the true fulfillment in life lie in the joy of the Torah, in the eternity of the Torah, and in the fulfillment of the holy commandments of the Lord contained therein.

Man often fools himself by pursuing a career as the end all and be all in life. He may try to fill the existential void by embracing false gods. Dr. Meiselman[2] (a contemporary rabbi and author) describes the kind of activities that are of consequence to Jewish women, and Jews in general:

> While housework forms a significant part of a woman's work, this does not mean that a woman was meant to define herself primarily in terms of this aspect of her job. When the prophet

---

[2] Dr. Moshe Meiselman, *Jewish Woman in Jewish Law* (Ktav Publishing House, 1978), p. 166.

Jonah was asked, "What is your work, and from which nation are you?" (Jonah 1:8), he answered: "I am a Hebrew and I fear the Lord, God of the Heavens, who has made sea and dry land" (Jonah 1:9). Jonah's self-definition was exclusively in terms of his religious activities. His other deeds did not contribute to his self-definition.

The self-definition of the Jewish woman should be that of the אשת חיל, "the virtuous woman," a woman who fears the Lord and performs acts of loving kindness. In a family-centered society (as adhered to by traditional Jews), the role of the female is obvious and clearly defined. The children are borne in her body and her relationship to the infant is one of the strongest emotional attachments known to man. All domestic activities revolve around the mother; she is the center of the home.

The male's role is somewhat more ambiguous. He essentially functions as breadwinner and protector of the family group. The male is, of course, also a parent. In fulfilling this role, however, he faces certain natural disadvantages. At best, the father can function in his role of parent only part-time. Thus, he cannot compete with the levels of warmth and closeness attained in the mother-child relationship.

The laws of the Torah come to equalize these innate disadvantages of the father. By emphasizing the male role outside the home (in the synagogue, schools, etc.), and by giving him a contrapuntal role in family life (balancing the mother's warmth with the father's demand for adherence to the Torah and additional commandments), true harmony is established.

Jewish tradition is exceedingly concerned about the religious well-being of the Jewish home. It is seen as the key to the survival of the Jews and Judaism. If a Jewish woman's *primary* dedication is to her career, her activities would certainly be considered inconsistent with the guidelines of our tradition. However, if a woman realizes that a career is only a means to an end (that end being the primary goal of building and maintaining a Jewish home according to Jewish ideals), then surely the pursuit of such a career would not be inconsistent with our tradition. In fact, because of modern-day mechanization of most household chores, many women find themselves with a good deal of free time which can be put to constructive use. Also, due to current economic pressures, a wife's second income is often necessary for the couple's survival. It is for these reasons that a good number of contemporary rabbis have tacitly sanctioned, even encouraged, women to work at least part time. They emphasize, however, that the woman's job shall in no way become her primary goal. She should always keep in mind that her work is but a means to an end, the end being the well-being of religious family life and Jewish survival.

The Torah has profound respect for the dignity and individuality of human beings. In Judaism, we believe that, to a large extent, a person has freedom of choice. Therefore, every Jew—male or female—has the option to do as he or she pleases. One may abide by the guidelines for living given by God, and trust that they will bring happiness and success, or one may do otherwise, and bear the consequences. Thus, women who wish to dedicate themselves to careers may do so. But they should bear in mind that it is often difficult to simultaneously maintain a happy and healthy religious family life and a successful and rewarding career.

In ancient Israel the two tribes of *Zebulun* and *Issachar* formed a partnership. Zebulun settled on the coast and engaged in commerce in order to support Issachar, who sat and toiled in the learning of Torah. Thus, Zebulun's wordly work became a religious dedication. The Torah endorses this relationship, saying: "Rejoice Zebulun in your goings out, and Issachar in your tents" (Deut. 33:18). Hence, Zebulun's work, the enabler, is considered of at least as high a religious quality as Issachar's, the performer. As we find in the Talmud Baba Batra 9a, ". . . the enabler of an act is greater than the performer."

A woman's ultimate task in life is to build a Jewish home.

The enabling role to this end applies to us all, but even more so to women. The Talmud states, "Greater is the reward given to women than the reward given to men" (Berachot 17a). *Aruch Ha-Shulchan, Yoreah Deah* 24b explains that the essential role of women in building the home is similar to that of Zebulun (whose reward is greater than that of Issachar). We learn from this that "enabling" is a primary Jewish act, and not a secondary level of performance.

Rambam's *Hilchot Ishut* 12:4 & 21:7, however, does not present a clear role definition for women. Thus Jewish law ends up mandating for women neither marriage [according to some authorities (text of Vilna Gaon of *Tosefta Yebamot* 8:2) a woman, unlike a man, is not required to marry; however, Rambam, in *Isurei Biah* 21:26, says, "A woman should not remain without a husband so that she not become suspect of immoral behavior"], nor procreation, nor specific household duties. The Rambam points out that while women are not required by law to pursue the above goals, throughout the generations, they have willingly and voluntarily taken upon themselves the burdens of the household. And the fact that they have done so has ensured the survival of the Jewish people to this day.

Thus, priest, levite, and Israelite, man and woman, are all dedicated to a single goal; that goal being the service of God, which can only be achieved if each party performs his or her own individual role.

Now we can analyze the second half of the verse in Genesis 3:16, when God said to Eve: ". . . and unto your husband shall be your longing, and he shall rule over you." On the surface, the verse seems to imply that man is the ruler of his wife, and that the relationship is one of master and subject. The majority of biblical commentaries, however, do not subscribe to this straightforward interpretation. For example, Rabbi Samson Raphael Hirsch, in his commentary on the Pentateuch, explains that because man is the breadwinner, the wife becomes dependent upon him.

The commentary Ha-Emek Davar interprets this verse as

the wife's perception of her husband. Because she always hopes and desires to find favor in the eyes of her husband, he is considered to "rule" her life. [Our rabbis say there are four תשוקות (desires) in the world: (1) The desire of a wife for her husband. (2) The desire of Cain and his followers to follow the evil inclination. (3) The desire of the earth for rain in order to benefit from it. (4) The desire of the Holy-One-Blessed-be-He for Israel to follow Him and walk in His path.]

The commentary Torah Temmimah adds that a woman always desires her husband when he is about to go on a trip. From this our rabbis learn that a man is obligated to have relations with his wife before he goes on a trip (Yebamot 62b). Furthermore, we learn that a woman desires in her heart, while a man will state his desire out loud. And for a woman not to speak of her desire is considered good manners (Erubin 100b).

Rashi's comments are as follows: *Teshukah* ("longing" in Hebrew) refers to sexual desire. Although a wife desires marital relations with her husband, she shall not have the boldness to demand it verbally. But the man may do so, and in this sense *he rules over her.*

Ramban (Nachmanides) quotes Rashi and adds that this modesty is a praiseworthy trait. He disagrees with Iben Ezra who states that we deduce from this verse that a wife should listen to her husband and follow his command. Ramban adds that *teshukah* refers only to longing and desire. Women were given sexual desire so that they have relations with their husbands, and not think of the pain of pregnancy and childbirth that may follow. To clinch his argument, the Ramban then asks, in essence, where have you seen a maid who desires and longs to buy herself a master, but, on the contrary, she tries to escape from her master?

All this brings us to conclude that God's words in this verse are not meant to imply male domination and female subordination. When Adam and Eve sinned against the

Lord's commandment and ate from the forbidden tree, God prescribed a punishment for each. To the woman, He said: "I will greatly multiply your pain and your travail, in pain you shall bring forth children, and unto your husband shall be your longing, and he shall rule over you." This entire verse of Genesis 3:16 comes to tell the woman that though, indeed, she will have pain in pregnancy and childbirth, this will not and should not keep her from having relations with her husband.

For those who favor checks and balance in biblical interpretations, the following analysis will be of particular interest. [As quoted above, the verse in Genesis 3:16 seems to, at least superficially, give man dominion over woman. Several verses later, in Genesis 3:20, Adam calls his wife "Eve because she was the mother of all living." A few chapters on, in Genesis 17:15, we find, "And God said to Abraham: As for your wife Sarai, you shall not call her name Sarai, but Sarah [shall be] her name." The change of name to Sarah signifies "as one who lays down the rule," the word "Sarah" connotes dominance. From here it would seem that Sarah, the woman, was given dominion over Abraham, the man.

Furthermore, in Genesis 17:4,5, God informed Abraham: "As for me behold My covenant [is] with you, and you shall be the father of a multitude of nations. Neither shall your name be called Abram any more, but your name shall be Abraham, for a father of multitude of nations I have made you." Here again we notice a reversal of roles. Abraham becomes "the father of multitude of nations," as Eve was "mother of all living."

If one carefully analyzes the four sources quoted above, the following interesting patterns emerge. When God gives man dominance over woman, He addresses the woman Eve directly. She is given the complimentary title of "mother of all living" however, by Adam, through God. When Sarah's name is changed—and God gives a woman dominance over a man—He does not speak directly to Sarah but instead tells her husband, Abraham. From God's actions in the above two instances, we can learn that the Almighty wishes woman to be kept modest at all times—as when receiving the honor of the name "mother of all living," and at the time of "dominance over man."

Adam as "ruler" may also be seen as simply representing human nature—wherein men often feel they have the right to dominate their wives. That may be so, but not as far as Jews are concerned. Both our intellectual pursuits and our ordinary daily conduct are derived from God's revelations through the patriarchs and the matriarchs. Thus our rabbis teach us that women are "the crowns of their husbands," and to be treasured as "the invaluable pearl."

Although neither man nor woman is meant to dominate the other, the role of the mother holds a special status in Judaism; the mother can and does exert great influence upon her entire household. The following serves as illustrations of the special significance of motherhood in Jewish culture.

Eve was called "the mother of all living" and anticipated in her name were the motherhoods of Sarah, Rebecca, Rachel, and Leah, the wives of the patriarchs. Adam, on the other hand, was never given the additional title of "the father of all living," but instead was only called "the first man." From this we can deduce that motherhood is a primary, more profound, and more lasting experience than fatherhood.

Traditional Jewish prayer, too, acknowledges the universal position of motherhood. When a Jew is sick and we recite the special prayers for recovery, we use the sick one's name and that of his/her mother. This tradition is based on King David's prayer for personal salvation, "And save the son of Your handmaid" (Ps. 86:16) (Zohar). The commentator Radak explains that King David tells God that he is His servant of his own free will, yet his development was influenced by the fact that his mother was God's devoted handmaid.

Moreover, the very essence of Judaism, the Jewish identity, is transferred only through the mother. If a Jewish woman marries a non-Jew and they have children, these children are still considered Jewish according to Jewish law. And even if her daughters go on to marry non-Jews, *their* children will still be considered Jewish. However, if a Jewish man marries a non-Jew, their children are automatically considered not to be Jewish. Hence, the influence of the Jewish woman has a far longer reach than that of the Jewish man, and the Lord Almighty saw fit to affirm this in his laws.

The Torah, in its infinite wisdom, was aware that people tend to respect their mothers more than their fathers, and so found it necessary to put the fathers first in the commandment: "Honor your father and your mother" (Exod. 20:12 & Deut. 5:16). However, the Torah was also aware that people fear their fathers more than their mothers, and therefore put the mother first in the commandment: "You shall fear every man his mother and his father" (Lev. 19:3). (However, both wife and children are to obey the words of the father. If a mother commands her child to do one thing and the father another, the child is to follow his father's command.)

The superior influence of women is best illustrated by the following parable: Once a pious man was married to a pious woman, but they had no children. They said, "We are unproductive to God," and were divorced. Later, the husband married an evil woman, and she turned him toward evil. The wife married an evil man, and she turned him toward good (see Gen. Rabbah 17; Yalkut Shimoni 2). Thus we see how strong and influential women can be.

In the Talmud Sanhedrin 110a, the following is quoted, "The wise among women builds her house . . ." (Proverbs 14:1). This proverb is applied to On ben Peleth's wife whose story is related in Midrash Numbers Rabbah 18:20: When Korach and the rest of his cohorts rebelled against Moses,

On ben Peleth's wife first tried reasoning with her husband. She told him he would gain nothing by participating in the rebellion; win or lose, his position would not be elevated. Finally, she fed him and gave him drinks to put him to sleep, thereby effectively preventing him from joining in the rebellion. And so when terrible punishment was later meted out to the rebellers, On ben Peleth was not among the victims. In fact, this wise woman, with her sound advice and superior insight, saved her husband's life.

Korach's evil wife, on the other hand, was able through her evil persuasion to convince her husband to rebel against Moses, and so led him and their family to an abysmal fate. And so she serves as a perfect example for the second half of the verse from Proverbs 14:1, ". . . but the foolish (woman) pulls it down with her own hands."

Thus we see how strong and influential women can be. As it is said: "A man is what his wife makes him." And, "Behind every great man there is an even greater woman."

Rabbi Samson Raphael Hirsch[3] develops and expounds on this topic:

> But just because the woman has not to acquire a calling and position for herself, she remains the nurse of all that is purely human in man. The great words with which the Father of humanity, as He fosters and watches over its departure, announces its ultimate salvation and ingathering after all the mistakes it has made in the course of its history, are: כי ברא ה׳ חדשה בארץ נקבה תסובב גבר "God creates something new on earth, a woman encircles a man" (Jeremiah 31:21). The calling and position for which a man has to struggle are really nothing but the foundation on which he has to build his life's work, and carry out his own share in the general task of humanity. And there is a danger that he may completely lose himself in this struggle, that is striving to acquire the means he will lose sight of his real vocation and completely forget the great goal and his

---

[3] Dayan Dr. I Grunfeld, *Judaism Eternal* (Soncino Press, London, 1956), Vol. 2, p. 52.

own task as a man, nay, that he will sacrifice and subordinate to these efforts what is genuinely human in himself. This is an error which can almost be regarded as the key to all the mistakes made in history. It is then the woman who leads him back to what is truly human in him. The riddle of history is solved with the domination of woman, with the restriction of the man to the sphere of the genuinely human which has been placed under the care of the woman.

Yes, women have a long lasting influence upon their husbands and children. They can lead them to a life of piety and fulfillment or, God forbid, to a life filled with wickedness and destruction.

Part Three

WOMEN'S EXEMPTIONS AND OBLIGATIONS IN COMMANDMENTS

I
The Commandments and Women

The Torah contains 613 commandments. Of these, 365 are negative commandments, as in "thou shall not," and 248 are positive ones, "thou shall." Almost all of the negative commandments are equally obligatory upon men and women. (A few obvious exceptions for women would be not rounding corners of hair on head, not shaving corners of beard, and not defiling oneself through contact with a dead body by male priests—Rambam, *Hilchot Avodat Kochavim* 12:3; Mishnah Kiddushin 1:7.)

Women, however, are not obligated to observe all the commandments. According to Rambam, there are fourteen positive commandments from which women are exempt. The first eight are time-bound, and the last six (9 through 14) are not. (Note: The term "time-bound" here refers to a commandment which has a specific time stipulation.) These positive commandments which women are not obligated to perform are:

1. Reciting of the *Shema* (affirmation of faith) twice daily.
2. Putting *tefillin* (phylacteries) on the head.
3. Putting *tefillin* on the arm.
4. Placing *tzitzit* (fringes) on four-cornered garments.
5. Counting the *Omer* (days from second night of Passover to Shavuot).

6. Dwelling in the *Succah* (booth).
7. Using the *lulab* in the festival of Succoth.
8. Hearing the *shofar* (ram's horn).
9. Learning and teaching the Torah.
10. Writing a Torah scroll.
11. Procreation.
12. Making one's wife happy during the first year of marriage.
13. Recitation of the priestly blessing by the male priests.
14. Circumcision.

In addition, women are exempt from the positive commandment of redeeming the first born.

The Talmud finds six time-bound, positive commandments for which both women and men are obligated. These are:

1. *Kiddush* (special blessing on wine) on the Sabbath. (See Berachot 20b.)
2. Fasting on *Yom Kippur* (Day of Atonement). (See Succah 28a.)
3. Eating of unleavened bread on Passover. (See Kiddushin 34b.)
4. Rejoicing on the Festivals. (See Kiddushin 34a.)
5. Assembling once in seven years. (See Kiddushin 34a.)
6. Sacrificing and eating the Passover lamb. (See Pesachim 91b.)

In addition, there are four rabbinically enacted time-bound, positive commandments that apply to both men and women. These are:

1. Lighting Chanukah lights. (See Sabbath 23a).
2. Reading the Book of Esther on Purim. (See Megillah 4a.)
3. Drinking four cups of wine on Passover. (See Pesachim 108a.)
4. Reciting *Hallel* (special thanksgiving prayer) on the night of Passover. (See Succah 38a.)

First we will deal with the general concept and implication of women being exempted from some time-bound, positive commandments. Afterwards, we will discuss a number of these commandments specifically.

Although halachic authorities do not generally give reasons for exemptions, various explanations have appeared now and again. Of these, the most simple explanation is that women are excused from time-bound, positive commandments because of their primary familial responsibilities which are both important and immense.

The majority of halachic authorities, however, do not offer any explanation for these exemptions. These questions are viewed under the category of questions to which the question "why?" cannot be applied. As will be elaborated later on, there are often instances in Jewish law where one cannot help but have faith in the Almighty's benevolence in decreeing such commandments. However, Talmud Baba Kama 15a does point out that the exemptions do not imply anything about the relative worth of men and women; both are of equal value.

As previously discussed, women are considered to have a spiritual edge over men, a fact that has been proven many times over the course of our long history. Let us now review some of the points made earlier regarding the spiritual status of women.

(1) Man was created from the dust of the earth, whereas woman was created from a human being who is at the top of the hierarchy of all other beings and things. (2) Among our matriarchs, Sarah is pointed to as being superior in prophecy to her husband Abraham. (3) Due to the merit of righteous Jewish women, were we set free from bondage in Egypt. (4) In the wilderness, our righteous women abstained from helping their husbands to sin against the Lord, refusing to yield their jewels to be used to make the golden calf. (5) The women of that same generation had such perfect faith in God that they refused to believe the spies' evil report about the Promised Land. Thus they did not rebel against the Lord but, on the contrary, their motto was, "Give us an inheritance in the Land of Israel." Their

husbands were not as virtuous. The men lost faith saying, "Let us appoint a leader and go back to Egypt."

Exodus Rabbah 28, commenting on the verse, "Thus shall you say to the house of Jacob [these are the women—Rashi], and you shall tell the children of Israel [these are men—Rashi]" (Exod. 19:3) and "... if you will indeed listen to My voice, and keep My covenant, then you will be Mine own treasure from among all the peoples . . ." (Exod. 19:5), asks why the women were to be told first of God's covenant. The answer is that they are more diligent in practicing the commandments, as recorded in Pesachim 48b.

From all this, it is evident that women are blessed with a deeper and stronger faith in God, and that they exist on a superior spiritual plane. The reader should be cautioned, however, that the term "superior" as used here is not meant to be taken in an absolute sense. What is meant is simply that women have a slight natural edge over man in their perception of God and their faith in Him. Men can attain this same level of spirituality by observing the commandments that are specifically geared to them. In Genesis Rabbah 44:1 and in Leviticus Rabbah 13:3, Rav says, "Precepts were given to Israel for the purpose of shaping mankind." Obviously, if men were given more precepts than women, it is because they are in greater need of shaping. One may then conclude that women are exempt from certain time-bound, positive commandments because they do not *need* them to come a step closer to God. Their inherent appreciation, understanding, and faith in God do not require such formal catalysts as tzitzit, tefillin, reciting the Shema, dwelling in a succah, and so on—all commandments which remind us of God's existence and His laws. The fact that men are obligated and women are not does not exist to appease women, nor is it to be seen as an unbearable insult to men. It is simply God's divine law given to us in his wisdom.

a. Tefillin:

Regarding tefillin (phylacteries) the Torah states: "And

these words shall be, which I command you this day, upon your heart. And you shall bind them for a sign upon your hand, and they shall be for frontlets between your eyes" (Deut. 6:6–8). "And you shall lay up these My words in your heart and in your soul and you shall bind them for a sign upon your hand, and they shall be for frontlets between your eyes" (Deut. 11:18).

And our rabbis deduce from the commandment of tefillin that women, in general, are exempt from the time-bound, positive commandments. Since the Torah states, ". . . teach them to your sons . . ." and not to your daughters, our rabbis learned that women are not obligated to learn Torah. In the Torah it is also written, ". . . so that the Torah of your God be upon your lips . . ." Therefore, anybody who is obligated in Talmud Torah is also obligated to don tefillin (Kiddushin 34a). (Note: This deduction is based on the text of the Parashat Shema, since it is stated there that the words of the Torah shall be taught to "your sons" and also that the words of the Torah shall be ". . . as a sign on your arm . . . and as a frontlet upon your head," thus obligating only the men to wear tefillin. And since donning tefillin is a time-bound, positive commandment for men only, any other time-bound, positive commandment will be obligatory for men, whereas women will be exempt from it as they are from the learning of the Torah.)

Tefillin (the actual phylacteries) are considered to be of the highest sanctity, second only to the sanctity of the Torah scroll. As such, there are special rules which govern how tefillin are to be treated and how one must act while wearing them. Rambam in *Hilchot Tefillin* 4:14, 15, 25 writes:

> One must touch the tefillin during the time that he wears them, for his mind must not deviate from them for even a moment. This is seen from the fact that their sanctity is greater than the sanctity of the tzitzit, since the tzitzit have the name of God only once and the tefillin have the ineffable name of God twenty-one times on the head and an equivalent number on the arm. Tefil-

lin requires cleanliness of the body. Thus one may not pass any air while he is wearing tefillin. Thus one may not sleep or doze while wearing tefillin. . . . The sanctity of tefillin is very great. For while tefillin are upon one's head and arms, he must be humble, God-fearing, and cannot be involved in laughter or idle talk, and cannot think evil thoughts.

The basic mitzvah of tefillin refers to their being worn all day long. However, since only a few exceptional models of sanctity and spirituality (examples would be Elisha Baal Kenafim [Talmud Sabbath 49a] and the Vilna Gaon) can adhere to such strict disciplines while wearing tefillin, ordinary men have taken to donning them only during prayer, the minimal period of time required.

Raavad believed there was no danger involved in the improper performance of most commandments—shofar, succah, lulab, and tzitzit among them. Thus he states that women may, if they wish, perform all the above commandments (and others) for which they are normally exempt, except for three commandments. The three commandments which Raavad believed women should not perform under any circumstances were: learning of the Torah, tefillin, and *semichah* (the ceremony of placing of the hands on the animal's head when it is being prepared for sacrifices in the Temple). Improper learning of the Torah (i.e. superficial learning) may lead to disasterous consequences due to false interpretations. Tefillin is a very sacred object which requires the utmost care in treatment, as expounded by Rambam above. Improper treatment of tefillin violates the very laws prescribed to treat this sacred object and so desecrates it. And improper performance of semichah results in violation of *meilah,* the laws governing the handling of the sacred objects.

Keeping all these specialized proscriptions in mind, our rabbis weighed the positive benefits against possible negative outcomes of misperformance and decided the risks, in these cases, were not worth the benefits. Therefore they discouraged women's optional performance of the above commandments. And women were to avoid wearing tefillin. Nevertheless, there have been a limited number of women throughout Jewish history who have worn tefillin. In the Talmud Eruvin 96a we find, "Michal, the daughter of Saul, put on tefillin and the sages did not protest." Upon closer scrutiny, however, we find Tosfot quoting the Talmud Yerushalmi Berachot 2:3, and Pesikta Rabati 22:112b which have a complete version of the Eruvin text:

> "And you shall teach it to your sons," but not to your daughters. He who is obligated to study is also obligated to don tefillin. Women, who are not obligated to study, are not obligated to don tefillin. A question was raised: But did not Michal the daughter of Saul put on tefillin and the sages did not protest? Rabbi Chizkiyahu in the name of Rabbi Abahu said ". . . the sages did protest."

The interdiction against a person's wearing clothing of the opposite sex is stated in Deut. 22:5: "The article of man should not be on a woman, nor should a man don woman's clothing, for whoever does these, it is an abomination before God." The wording of this verse poses some difficulty and serves as the basis for a Tannaitic dispute in the Braitha as to the exact definition of the biblical prohibition (Talmud Nazir 59a; Sifri, Deut. 22:5):

> "A man's article should not be upon a woman . . ." What is this informing us? If it simply tells us that a man may not wear a woman's garment, nor a woman wear a man's garment, it is already stated (at the end of the verse) "for whoever does these, it is an abomination, etc.," and there is no abomination here. [Note: The word "abomination" is used for forbidden intercourse; what is meant here by "no abomination" is that the mere act of putting on the garments is not wrong; what is wrong is the mingling of men and women leading to forbidden intercourse.] Rather, a man should not dress in a woman's

garment and sit among women, nor a woman should wear a man's garment and sit among men.

Rabbi Eliezer Ben Yaakov said, "From where [do we derive] that a woman may not go out to war with weapons? From where it states in the Torah, "The articles of a man should not be on a woman, nor should a man don a woman's clothing . . .""

From this, we also learn that a man should not adorn himself as women do. The extent to which this prohibition applies has been a traditional matter of dispute among halachic authorities through the ages. Most authorities agree with Rabbi Eliezer who defines "man's" and "woman's" clothing as that which each sex wears or does specifically for beauty and adornment. Thus, by definition, items worn for utilitarian purposes are excluded. In addition, items worn for beauty and adornment are themselves only forbidden when the intention of the wearer is to pass as a member of the opposite sex. However, wearing such items for protection against rain and cold is permitted.

The Shulchan Aruch forbids a man to look at himself in the mirror out of sheer vanity, since that is a female cosmetic practice; but does allow him to use a mirror for many motives such as shaving or cutting his hair. Rambam in *Hilchot Avodah Zarah* 12:10 rules in favor of Rabbi Eliezer Ben Yaakov's definition of tweezing hair or dyeing gray hair spoken of in the Talmud Makot 20a and Sabbath 94b as being a woman's practice. For this same reason, men are forbidden to remove hair from their bodies' private parts.

Similarly, Targum Yonatan Ben Uziel derives the prohibition of wearing tzitzit and tefillin by women from Deut. 22:5. Tzitzit and tefillin are simply seen as male garments which should not be worn by a woman.

Moreover, the tefillin's function is to serve as an אות, a sign, for men—to remind them to perform God's commandments and so bring them closer to God. Again, the

Torah did not deem it necessary, for women to be so dramatically reminded of God's commandments as it was taken for granted that they are, by their very nature, closer to God and mindful of His ways. Rambam's remarks in *Hilchot Tefillin* 4:25 imply that tefillin inspire humility and fear of God in one's heart and mind. Because women by nature are known to be modest and humble in character, and fearful of God, they do not need the extra inspiration one gets from tefillin.

Thus the majority of halachic authorities throughout the ages have prohibited women from wearing tefillin. This view is also held by the Shulchan Aruch and Rama in the code of Jewish law.

b. Tzitzit

The biblical commandment for wearing tzitzit (fringes) is found in Numbers 15:38–40: "And they shall make themselves fringes in the corners of their garments throughout their generations and [that] they shall put with the fringe of [every] corner a thread of blue. And it shall be unto you for a fringe, that you may look upon it and remember all the commandments of the Lord and do them, that you go not about after your own heart and your own eyes after which you use to go astray. That you may remember and do all My commandments and be holy unto your God."

In Talmud Menachot 43a our rabbis teach that the priests, the levites, the Israelites, the proselytes, the women, and the servants are all obligated in the commandment of tzitzit. But Rabbi Shimon exempts women and servants because this is a time-bound, positive commandment. It can be considered "time-bound" in two ways. First, as the Scripture states, "... you shall see them ..." we learn that the obligation of tzitzit exists only during the day (and not at night). (See Rambam *Hilchot Tzitzit* 3:7.) Second, according to Rabbenu Tam and Rosh the obligation of tzitzit depends upon the type of garment worn. If the garment is one generally designated for use by day, it would require tzitzit whether it is worn during the day or at night. But if the garment is one designated for night use, it is altogether exempt from tzitzit, even if worn during the day. At any rate, through either categorization, the mitzvah of tzitzit remains a time-bound, positive commandment (see Tosfot Kiddushin 34a).

The commandment of tzitzit is optional even for men. It is not an absolute requirement, as are such commandments as shofar or tefillin. A man is only required to wear tzitzit when he wears a four-cornered garment. Yet, Rambam in *Hilchot Tzitzit* 3:11 states:

> ... though a man is not required to buy a tzitzit and wrap himself in it, so that he will perform a mitzvah of tzitzit, it is not fitting for a pious man to exempt himself from this mitzvah, rather, he should always strive to wrap himself in a garment which requires tzitzit, so that he will fulfill the commandment. At the time of prayer he should make a greater effort. It is unbecoming to a great Torah scholar to pray when he is not wrapped in a tzitzit.

Thus, for women, the commandment of tzitzit is doubly optional: First, it is a time-bound, positive commandment. And second, the commandment itself is an optional one—wherein a person is only obligated when he wears a four-cornered garment. To wear tzitzit on a regular basis is an act of extra piety which all men have accepted upon themselves, and women did not. (This is not the case with all time-bound, positive commandments. Women did, for instance, accept the commandment of shofar.)

However, according to Rama, "If women wish they may wear a tzitzit and recite the blessing thereof as in other time-bound, positive commandments, but it might appear as *yoharah* [explanation in the next paragraph]. Therefore, they should not do so, for even a man is not required to wear a tzitzit" (*Orah Hachaim* 17:2).

Yoharah refers to acts which may indicate a false religious pride, as in religious exhibitionism, and it applies to both men and women. (For a more in-depth discussion of *Yoharah,* refer to Meam Loez on Lev. 11:4-7, Talmud Berachot 17b, Pesachim 55a, and Succah 26b.) The laws of *yoharah* basically dictate that before a person attempts "extra piety," he should first see to it that he is proficient in the most basic areas of religious observance.

A woman who is motivated to adhere to the ways of Torah, should first become proficient in the more basic areas of religious observance before moving to the observance of the doubly-optional commandment of tzitzit or other optional commandments. The commandment of tzitzit serves as a reminder to know and to remember the Holy-One-Blessed-be-He and to do His commandments. Men are admonished to wear this reminder so that they will not fall into the trap of "the eyes see and the heart desires." Women, on the other hand, have better control of their desires and need no such strong reminders. What is required of them is simply to dress modestly and act modestly, as is befitting a King's daughter. The purpose of such modesty in dress and behavior is twofold: In one sense, it can be seen as a substitute for tzitzit (modest dress is women's tzitzit as it were), and secondly, it serves to minimize the arousal of indecent thoughts in men's minds.

c. Reciting the Shema:

Men are obligated to recite the *Shema* twice daily. The prayer's major theme is the affirmation of God's unity. שמע ישראל ה׳ אלהינו ה׳ אחד "Hear, O Israel: The Lord our God, the Lord is one" (Deut. 6:4). The Shema also discusses putting on tefillin and wearing tzitzit as quoted earlier, as well as remembering, doing, teaching, and learning the commandments of the Lord, and walking in His path. As discussed, women are not obligated to wear neither tefillin nor tzitzit.

And the major theme of the Shema—the unity of God—had already been unanimously declared by women when they refused to participate in creating the golden calf. (At that time, women, in essence, demonstrated their fear of God and testified to His unity.) Nevertheless, some authorities (Bach on Tur Orah Hachaim 70 sub nashim, and Aruch Hashulchan 70:1) maintain that women are obligated to recite at least the first verse (the one quoted above) from the parashat Shema, and so continually reaffirm their devotion and allegiance to God.

One may ask why the priests and levites—who, like women, exist on a slightly higher spiritual plane than the general population—are not also exempted from these commandments? The answer to this question lies with the special position priests and levites occupy within the community. Namely, they are in a position of power. Unfortunately, human nature being what it is, people in power are more likely to use their position to do wrong than good. For this reason, the priests and levites were given extra commandments to serve as constant reminders that they, too, are subject to God's will.

A clear example of a position of power necessitating extra commandments would be Israel's kings. A Jewish king, by law, is required to observe a number of specific restrictions. He is not to take too many wives nor amass too much wealth, lest his heart be turned away from the Lord. He is to have a Torah scroll at his side and read it often so that the fear of the Lord fills his heart and leads him to follow His commandments. Finally, he is to put the Lord before him at all times, as revealed by King David: "I have set the Lord before me always, because He is at my right hand I shall not falter" (Ps. 16:8).

d. The Succah (Tabernacle, Booth):

Jews are commanded to dwell in booths for seven days, to hold the *lulab* (branches of palm trees), and to rejoice before the Lord our God. As it is written:

On the fifteenth day of the seventh month when you have gathereth in the fruits of the land, you shall keep the feast of the Lord seven days, on the first day [shall be] a solemn rest, and on the eighth day [shall be] solemn rest. And you shall take to you on the first day the fruit of the goodly trees, branches of palm trees, and boughs of thick trees and willows of the brooks and you shall rejoice before the Lord Your God seven days (Lev. 23:39-40).

The holiday of Succoth comes to teach us about the transient nature of our lives on earth and remind us of our ultimate dependence on God. At the very time that a man is ready to gather his harvest, he is commanded to set aside all earthly works and engage exclusively in the service of God. The message is that man's earthly endeavors are of no consequence; the real fruit and harvest of his labors come from performing God's work.

Women, on the other hand, are not totally immersed in the worldly pursuits of earning a living. As explained by Rabbi S. R. Hirsch, women function as "priests" in their own miniature sanctuaries, their homes. Because of their special sensibilities, they are constantly aware of the existence of God and cognizant of His concern for the human race. Therefore, unlike men who require specific commandments to relieve them of their earthly cares, women need not be distracted from their everyday work/service in their miniature sanctuaries. They become actively involved in the celebration of the holiday by extending their priestly role in the home—i.e. by involving themselves in all necessary holiday preparations. Through their dedicated ministrations, they enhance the family's enjoyment of the holiday, thus creating an environment which realizes its ultimate purpose—namely, the realization of our dependence on God and the transient nature of this world.

Women are obligated in the time-bound, positive commandment of rejoicing on the Festivals. And husbands, in fact, have a special obligation to ensure their wives' "rejoicing" by buying them garments, jewels, and other presents according to their financial means and the custom of the land (Talmud Pesachim 109a, Shulchan Aruch, Orah Hachaim 529:2). The reason festivals do not fall under the rule of women's exemption from time-bound, positive commandments is that each Festival is based upon particular events that pertain equally to women and men. On Passover, for instance, we celebrate our redemption from Egyptian bondage. Women, too, were freed from bondage at that time. On Pentecost, we celebrate receiving the Torah from God. Naturally, the Torah was given to women as well as men. On Succoth, we celebrate the fact that God protected us while we lived in booths during our journeys in the wilderness. Obviously, women, too, were protected by the booths. This same line of reasoning can be applied to eating unleavened bread on Passover, to sacrificing and eating the Passover lamb, and the four rabbinically enacted time-bound, positive commandments. Rashi, however, in Kiddushin 24a, suggests that since women are included in the negative commandment of not eating leavened bread on Passover, they are also included in the positive commandment of eating unleavened bread on Passover.

Women are obligated to light Chanukah candles and to hear the reading of the Megillah on Purim since they, too, were involved in these miracles. More than just involved, women played an integral part in the miracles that occurred; Yehudit is the heroine of Chanukah and Queen Esther of Purim. Moreover, women in general were included in the decrees of spiritual annihilation and physical destruction during these respective periods.

With regard to fasting on Yom Kippur—since we are all guilty of committing sins during the course of the year, and we all need to do repentance, it is incumbent upon both men and women to observe this commandment.

Sometimes, when a negative aspect of a commandment applies to women, they are also required to observe its positive counterpart. For example, the commandment to sanctify the Sabbath is a positive commandment observed by saying *Kiddush* (special recital of blessing over the wine). However, since the negative commandment not to perform labor on the Sabbath applies to both men and women, as part of their observance of the Sabbath, women are required to observe the time-bound, positive commandment of saying Kiddush as well. As the Talmud Berachot 20b states, "whoever is obligated in observing the Sabbath [by not doing work], is also obligated in remembering [sanctifying] it [by saying Kiddush]."

From our previous discussions, one may well conclude that the exemption of women from some of the positive commandments in no way implies inferiority on their part, but is rather due to their superior spirituality. Even though not all such positive commandments were analyzed here, we may safely assume the others do not, in any way, reflect poorly upon women. In fact, some of these positive commandments—such as making one's wife happy during the first year of marriage—do not apply to women for obvious reasons. The learning and teaching of Torah will be discussed in a separate section later on.

Rabbi S. R. Hirsch writes[1] that the nature of man's day-to-day activities require extra commandments to provide him with proper spiritual balance. Hirsch first establishes the problems that the breadwinner encounters while pursuing his career to earn a livelihood by commenting on verse 3 of chapter 8 of Deuteronomy:

> The worry to provide bread for wife and child is, in itself, such a justified incentive for our activities, that it easily tends to drive all other considerations out of sight, as soon as we believe that we, and we alone, have to provide for the existence of ourselves

---

[1] Rabbi S. R. Hirsch, *Pentateuch* (Judaica Press, LTD, Gateshead, 1982), pp. 139–140.

and those dependent on us. As soon as we believe every acquisition that we wrest from Nature and our contemporaries insure our and their existence no matter how that acquisition had been obtained, whether thereby we had cared for the laws of God and kept to the path He had indicated, or whether only by clear deft handling we have secured the "bread" without giving a thought as to whether God would agree with these means. And where this looking on one's own human powers alone having to provide "bread" does not lead us away from the path of what is right and where our duty lies. It is still inclined to make us think of providing beyond the immediate necessities toward an ever-widening future. We think we have never done enough to satisfy our imagined duty, and talk ourselves into believing we have not discharged it unless we have acquired beforehand the means of existence for the whole of the future and for that of our children and grandchildren, and so we make the "worry of providing Bread" into an unlimited, breathless chase after income which denies any time for interest in purely intellectual and spiritual matters.

Hirsch discusses the concept of women's exemption from the time-bound positive commandments in his comments on verse 43 of chapter 23 of the Leviticus. Basically, he expresses a view about women very similar to the one presented earlier. He writes:[2]

> Torah did not impose these מצות on women because it did not consider them necessary to be demanded from women. All מצות שהזמן גרמא (time-bound positive commandments) are meant, by symbolic procedures, to bring certain facts, principles, ideas, and resolutions, afresh to our mind from time to time to spur us on afresh and to fortify us to realize them to keep them. God's Torah takes it for granted that our women have greater fervor and more faithful enthusiasm for their God-serving calling, and that this calling runs less danger in their case than in that of men from the temptations which occur in the course of

---
[2] *Ibid.*, p. 712.

business and professional life. Accordingly, it does not find it necessary to give women these repeated spurring reminders to remain true to their calling, and warning against weakness in their business life. Thus, at the very origin of the Jewish people, God's foresight did not find it necessary to ensure their bond with Him by giving women some permanent symbols in place of Mila (circumcision) for men. So, also at the Lawgiving on Sinai, God reckoned first of all (Ex. 19:3) on the faith and devotion of women. So, also the Jewish Nation has established the fact—and all our generations have inherited it—that in all the sins into which our nation has sunk, it has been בשכר נשים צדקניות, the faithfulness of our women to their convictions and sense of duty which has preserved and nurtured the seed of revival and return.

Eliyahu Kitov, a renowned Israeli author, while establishing the superiority of the Jewish woman, takes an interesting approach to this concept of women's exemption from time-bound, positive commandments. In his book, *The Jew and His Home*,[3] Kitov writes:

> For not only women are exempt from certain commandments in the Torah. It sometimes happens that men too are exempted from some commandments. For example, if a man is already engaged in the performance of a commandment and a second commandment presents itself, then he is exempt from performing the second commandment. In some cases commandments become obligatory which involve the overriding of other commandments. A classical example of this in the Talmud is the case of a Nazir (see Numbers 6:2, a man who is, amongst other things, forbidden to come into contact with dead bodies), who is at the same time a High Priest (for whom such contact is still more stringently forbidden) about to slaughter the Passover-offering and to circumcise his son (two commandments the transgression of which involves the most severe of penalties). If

---

[3] A. E. Kitov, *The Jew and His Home* (Shengold Publishing Co. New York, 1963), pp. 66–67.

he learns of the death of one of his nearest relatives, he is not allowed to attend to the actual burial, since his status forbids him to come into contact with dead bodies. But if he finds an unburied corpse for whom there is no one else to care, he is not only permitted but duty-bound to violate his status as a Nazir and as a priest, to disregard the Passover-offering and the circumcision of his son, to disregard every other commandment and to perform this one commandment. His exemption from all other commandments is certainly no sign of inferiority, he is exempt from them because a more important duty rests upon him at that moment.... From this it can readily be understood that if two persons are equally duty-bound to observe commandments, and one of them is exempted from some, this exemption is due to another duty which rests upon him and which does not rest upon his friend. And the exemption proves that he has a more important task to do which cannot be done except by him.

Thus, women, basically equal to men with regard to all the commandments of the Torah, but exempt from some which have time-limits, is proved thereby to be superior, for the special tasks which are hers, must be the reason for her exemption.

It should be emphasized that most authorities agree women may perform the commandments from which they are exempted, but the question of whether they may recite the appropriate blessings before performing these commandments is very controversial.

Interestingly, women throughout the ages have accepted upon themselves a number of time-bound, positive commandments such as shofar and lulab, and according to most halachic authorities, these commandments now have the status of an accepted custom or vow for women.

Thus, women's exemption from certain obligations does not exclude them from performing those obligations. The value of a commandment lies in its divine command, as the essence of the Jewish faith lies in living in accordance with divine law. For a man or woman, "divine law" means the imperative given to him or to her.

There are three duties specifically enjoined upon the Jewish woman by Divine command. The first of these is the kindling of the Sabbath candles. Both men and women are obligated in the lighting of Sabbath candles; however, in view of the fact that the woman is the one who is more commonly found at home attending to household affairs, she is privileged to perform this duty (Rambam, Hilchot Sabbath 5:3). Even if the husband desires to light the candles himself, his wife takes precedence and he fulfills his obligation through her.

The second obligation is the taking of *Challah* (a portion of dough). The Bible commands that the first part of dough used in baking be set aside and consecrated to the priests in the Holy Temple. After the destruction of the Temple, we continue to symbolically offer this part by breaking off a small piece of dough and throwing it into a fire or burning it in the oven. And for the same reason as cited above—because women are homemakers—this commandment was specifically given to them.

The third obligation assigned to women are the laws of *niddah,* or marital separation. Jewish law forbids all sexual contact between husband and wife during the wife's menstrual period and for seven days thereafter. Before resumption of intercourse, the wife must immerse herself in the *mikvah,* a special type of ritual bath. The laws of *niddah* will be dealt with in detail further on in the section on "Family Purity."

2
The Study of the Torah by Women

The commandment of teaching Torah was explicitly given to us in the following biblical verse: ושננתם לבנך ודברת בם בשבתך בביתך ובלכתך בדרך ובשכבך ובקומך "And you shall teach them [the words of Torah] diligently to your children, and you shall talk of them when you sit in your house and when you walk by the way and when you lie and when you rise up" (Deut. 6:7). The Talmud Kiddushin 29b understands the word לבנך (to your sons) to imply that the Torah is to be taught to "sons" and not "daughters."

The Talmud goes on to deduce from the verse that follows: ולמדתם אתם את בניכם לדבר בם בשבתך בביתך ובלכתך בדרך ובשכבך ובקומך "And you shall teach them [the words of Torah] to your children, to talk of them when you sit in your house and when you walk by the way and when you lie down and when you rise up" (Deut. 11:19), that one whom others are commanded to teach is also commanded to teach himself or learn from others, and one whom others are not commanded to teach is not commanded to teach himself or learn from others. Thus, clearly the Talmud imposes no obligation to teach Torah to women nor are women under any obligation to learn Torah or to teach Torah to themselves. All major halachic authorities subscribe to this notion. (See Shulchan Aruch Yoreah Deah 246:6; Tur Yoreh Deah 246:6; Rambam, Talmud Torah 1:13; Semag, Positive

Commandments 12; Rif, Kiddushin 29b; Rosh, Kiddushin 29b; Palestinian Talmud, Berachot 2:7 and Eruvin 10:1.)

The teaching and learning of the Torah embraces two commandments. One is the general מצוות תלמוד תורה (the commandment of teaching and learning Torah) which can be paraphrased as מצוות חנוך (the commandment of "essential" education) as expressed by the term ולמדתם in the second verse, "and you shall teach them." The purpose of this commandment is to familiarize every Jew with the basic tenets of Judaism, and so make it possible for everyone to live a life of Torah.

The other commandment is expressed by the ושננתם as used in the first verse, meaning "and you shall teach them diligently." Though this term encompasses the general commandment of education, it specifically points to an in-depth level of study. Rashi, elaborating on the meaning of ושננתם, says the term denotes "sharpness." One should learn till the words of the Torah become so sharp (ready) in one's tongue that if asked a halachic question, one need not stammer but can answer immediately. Obviously, many years of devoted and diligent study are required to attain so high a level of expertise.

The authorities generally agree that women are obligated in the commandment of "essential" education, but not in the commandment of in-depth, long-term study. The commandment of "essential" education is found in Genesis, as given to the first Jew, Abraham: כי ידעתיו למען אשר יצוה את־בניו ואת־ביתו אחריו ושמרו דרך ה' לעשות צדקה ומשפט למען הביא ה' על־ אברהם את אשר־דבר עליו "For I have known him, to the end that he may command his sons and his household after him, that they may keep the way of the Lord to do righteousness and justice to the end that the Lord may bring upon Abraham [that] which He has spoken to him" (Gen. 18:19).

Minhat Hinuch interprets "his household" to mean "his daughters," and so we learn that this commandment which refers to "essential" learning and teaching of Torah applies equally to the sons and daughters of our father Abraham.

The commandment of "essential" education for all Jews is further evidenced by the following: "And Moses called to all Israel and said to them: Hear, O' Israel, the statutes and the ordinances which I speak in your ears this day, that you may learn them, and observe to do them" (Deut. 5:1). In this verse, Moses addresses "all Israel"—both men and women—thereby obligating them to study and know God's Torah so that they may perform His commandments. For, as we learn in Abot 2:5, "The ignorant cannot be fearful of sin nor can they be pious." In addition, Tosfot on Talmud Sotah 21b quoting the Talmud Hagigah 3a comments on the following verse, "Assemble the people, men and women and children, and your stranger within your gates so that they will hear [understand] and so that they will learn and they will fear the Lord, your God and they will keep in order to perform all the words of this Torah" (Deut. 31:12). The commentary explains that women are specifically mentioned here to show that they are obligated to hear the commandments so that they will know them and fulfill them properly.

The author would like to include here the famous discussion in Talmud Sotah 20a regarding Torah study by women. "Ben Azzai said that a man must teach his daughter the law. . . . Rabbi Eliezer said that he who teaches his daughter the law is considered as if he taught her *tiflut*." [Note: Other Tannaim (Talmudic sages) also disagreed with Ben Azzai's view (Hagigah 3a).]

There are two major interpretations of the term *tiflut*. Most authorities interpret it to mean "trivial and irrelevant things." The second interpretation says it refers to "immorality." Rashi on Sotah 21b understands the term *tiflut* to mean lechery, and explains that according to Rabbi Eliezer, if a woman is taught Torah, she will acquire wisdom or subtlety and thus know how to conduct immoral affairs without being found out.

Rambam adopts the first interpretation (of triviality) and goes on to say that certain areas of study are so inherently profound, they can be understood by only a limited number of people. This, however, is not the case with the Torah, as quoted in Hilchot Yesodei Ha-Torah 4:13, "It is accessible to all, young and old, men and women, those with great minds and those with limited ones." Nevertheless, Rambam in Hilchot Talmud Torah 1:13 states that since women in general are not ready to dedicate themselves completely to Torah study, their Torah knowledge will be superficial. And it is exactly in such superficial knowledge that the danger lies. Superficial learning would keep women from appreciating the profundity of Jewish knowledge, and they would then come to consider it trivial and irrelevant.

Superficial knowledge is dangerous in any area of endeavor. It can easily lead to misunderstanding, misinterpretation, and misdirection on the parts of both men and women. The laws of family purity is one example of an intricate system of Jewish laws wherein the woman's judgement is relied upon. If a woman's knowledge in this area is superficial, she may inadvertently make halachic decisions that violate these very important laws and so lead to immoral behavior.

The two seemingly contradictory statements about women's study made by Rabbi Eliezer and Ben Azzai can be resolved as follows. Rabbi Eliezer's negative statement regarding teaching "the law" to women should be seen as referring only to the study of the Talmud. Rabbi Eliezer does not object to women learning the Bible nor Jewish laws (like family purity) in order to know how to conduct their lives. As such, Rabbi Eliezer's opinion does not contradict Ben Azzai's view of "teaching Torah" to women.

Furthermore, in order to better understand Ben Azzai's statement, we must place it in its proper context. For this we need to analyze the discussion directly preceding it in the Talmud Sotah 20a. In the preceding paragraph, the Mishnah talks about the ritual pertaining to a married woman suspected of adultery. The Mishnah states that if the woman has any merits, her heavenly punishments will be deferred proportional to those merits. And immediately thereafter Ben Azzai states, "... from here we see that a man shall teach his daughter Torah . . ." (the reason obviously being that by learning Torah one accumulates merits).

It is inconceivable that Ben Azzai would recommend Torah-learning for improper purposes—i.e. in order to delay punishment of someone accused of committing one of the three cardinal sins ("cardinal sins" refer to sins where a person is to sacrifice his/her life rather than commit the sin). Rather, Ben Azzai's statement should be read as a concerned warning. A father is to teach his daughter Torah so that she will know the fear of God and comport herself in a pious manner. Thus will she be able to avoid any situation which might put her under suspicion of adultery. And if, perchance, she is suspected of adultery, she will be confident that her piety will prove her guiltless and will not hesitate to conform to the prescribed ritual. This interpretation is in agreement with Tosfot on Sotah 21b, where Tosfot concludes that women are obligated to hear the commandments in order to know them and to fulfill them, and not in order to know them so as to acquire merits to defer their punishments.

When looked at in this vein, we may even better understand Rabbi Eliezer's statement and its purpose in coming directly after the words of Ben Azzai. In essence, Rabbi Eliezer is saying that if a man teaches his daughter Torah with the thought in mind that her punishment will be deferred in the event she sins, this would constitute an abuse of the Torah and will lead to immorality. In this case, Rashi's interpretation of the word *tiflut* as "lechery" coincides with the above interpretation.

Learning the Torah in depth is an optional activity for women. If a woman studies Torah, it is considered meritorious, but not as meritorious as when a man studies Torah. Rambam in *Hilchot Talmud Torah* 1:13 explains: "A woman who studies Torah is rewarded, but not to the same extent as is a man, for she is not commanded and anyone who does that which he is not commanded to do, does not receive the same reward as one who is commanded, but a lesser reward."

Rabbi Meir said: "How do we know that even a gentile who learns Torah is to be considered on par with the high priest? It is because the verse in the Scripture says: 'Which a person shall do to live by them' (Lev. 18:5). It does not say 'priest' or 'levite' or 'Jew' but rather person. This teaches us that even a gentile who learns Torah is to be considered on the same level as a high priest" (Sanhedrin 59a). It has been said with regard to Rabbi Meir's statement that the gentile does not receive the reward of the obligated performer, but rather that of the non-obligated performer (which is less), for Rabbi Hanina said: "Greater is the reward of he who performs out of obligation than he who performs not out of obligation."

Rabbi Chaim Yoseph David Azulay (*Chidah,* as he is commonly known) was puzzled by the fact that the Talmud described so positively the immense scholarship of Bruriah, the wife of Rabbi Meir and the daughter of Rabbi Hananiah ben Teradion. He reasoned that the command of the Sages not to teach women Torah was merely a warning against teaching women who were not sufficiently motivated. The Sages were cognizant of the fact that women were not generally involved in intellectual pursuits at the time and therefore warned against a shallow involvement. This warning was not meant to be taken as a legal prohibition, however, and did allow for motivated women to pursue their interest in learning Torah. Looked at in this light, the sage's dictum also allows for a change in the popular attitude about women's motivation. As evidenced by our present generation, whereas a growing number of women are embracing intellectual pursuits, their "motivation" and thus suitability for Torah learning would hardly be in question.

All authorities agree that women are required to learn those areas of the Torah that are necessary for their proper performance of the commandments. Rabbi Israel Meir ha-Cohen (d. 1933), better known as Chafetz Chaim, in his work *Likutei Halachot to Sotah* 20a, p. 11a, deemed it necessary to make the following observation:

> It would seem to me that this (Rambam's law) not only applies at those times of history when everyone lived in the place of his ancestors and the ancestral tradition was very strong for each individual and this motivated him to act in the manner of his forefathers. . . . However, nowadays, when the tradition of our fathers has become very weakened and we find people who do not live close to the parental environment, and especially that there are those who have been given a secular education, certainly it is required to teach them the entire Bible, the ethical writings of our sages, etc. so that the principles of our holy faith will be strong for them. Otherwise, God forbid, they may deviate from the path of God, and violate all the precepts of the Torah.

The Chafetz Chaim seems to be speaking directly to our generation. In our present society, with its overbearing emphasis upon secular knowledge, it is incumbent upon every Jew—man and woman alike—to keep his or her Jewish education on par with, if not at a higher level than, his or her secular education.

Rabbi Zalman Sorotzkin (d. 1966) in his work *Moznayim la-Mishpat,* 42 reasoned along the same lines as the Chafetz Chaim. He claimed that, nowadays, if women are not taught Torah, they will be led to immorality through the influence of the corrupted cultures that surround us.

Rabbi Avraham Dujenski adds that because morally wrong philosophies and beliefs are so prevalent in today's society, every type of Torah-learning that can bring about character development, fear of God, and the love of God is to be considered obligatory for both men and women. Accordingly, women nowadays have an obligation to learn Torah in order to perfect their attributes and guard themselves against impious values and trends.

Contemporary Orthodox Jewry has more or less recognized the need for women to be knowledgeable of Torah Judaism. Much thanks and gratitude is owed to Sarah Schenirer who pioneered the idea of seminaries of higher Jewish education or *beth yaakovs* for women.

Nevertheless, the majority of halachic authorities hold that women should not be taught the Talmud. A number of authorities grant that there is no prohibition against a woman's learning the Talmud by herself—as did Bruriah and several others throughout our history. In Exodus 19:3 it is written: "Thus shall you say to the house of Jacob, and tell to the children of Israel." Rashi, quoting the *Mechilta,* says that "to the house of Jacob" refers to the women—that you shall talk to them with soft words. "And tell to the children of Israel" refers to men—who shall be taught the detailed and minute laws. Thus, we see further evidence for the claim that women are to be taught the general laws necessary for their observance of the commandments.

Study of the Talmud requires much dedication and devotion, as well as a long-term commitment to learning the Talmud in depth. A superficial knowledge of the Talmud would not only be useless, but could also be misleading. Since women have other far more important commitments, and therefore do not have the time to learn the Talmud properly (i.e. in depth), they are exempt from Talmud study.

Another possible reason why women are not obligated to study the Talmud is that the Talmud is so fascinating, one can become totally absorbed in it, to the extent of neglecting other vital tasks. In the Talmud Pesachim 4a we learn that a student of the Talmud shall not begin to study on the fourteenth day of the month of *Nisan* (the month of the Passover holiday), lest he become so absorbed in his studies that he forget to search for unleavened bread. Just as searching for unleavened bread on the night of the fourteenth day of *Nisan* is so important that it overrides a man's obligation to study the Talmud, so too, a woman's obligations all year round are so important that they override the option of studying the Talmud. Once again, all halachic authorities concur that women should be knowledgeable of the basic principles in Judaism and learn the laws pertaining to them and their daily conduct.

Certainly, in Judaism, we have nothing to hide. Our God is just, His Torah is just, and His Prophets and His Sages are just. The Torah is available to everyone. It is the Jewish ideal for every Jew to be well-versed and knowledgeable of God's laws so that he or she can properly fulfill His precepts. If our Sages restricted (or, as some authorities understand it, warned against) engaging in the study of certain areas of our rich tradition, they did so with the best of intentions, as explained through various reasons known to us and many unknown to us.

3

Women and Prayer

The commandment of prayer is derived from the biblical verse: "לאהבה את־ה' אלהיכם ולעבדו בכל־לבבכם ובכל נפשכם "To love the Lord your God, and to serve Him with all your heart and with all your soul" (Deut. 11:13). The Talmud (Taanit 2a; Arachim 11a) defines "service of the heart" as prayer. Rambam, in *Hilchot Tefillah* 1:1 writes that daily prayer is a positive biblical commandment given to us by the Scripture through the phrase: ועבדתם את ה' אלהיכם "And you shall serve the Lord your God" (Exod. 23:25). עבדה (service) is taken to mean "prayer" from the aforementioned verse, ". . . to serve Him with all your heart" (Deut. 11:13).

Our model of prayer is Channah, mother of Samuel, of whom it is written, "But Channah, she was speaking in her heart, only her lips were moving, and her voice was not heard" (I Samuel 1:13). As mentioned above, prayer in Judaism is denoted in terms of "service of the heart." It is a highly personal communication, one in which every Jew bears his innermost desires and emotions before the Lord. As revealed by the Psalmist: "A prayer of the afflicted man when he is troubled and pours forth his supplication before God" (Ps. 102:1). And, as we learn from Channah's example, private prayers are best offered in silence.

It should be pointed out that the term "prayer" as used here specifically refers to the daily *shemoneh-esreh* (the eighteen blessings of the *Amidah*) in the regular morning and afternoon prayers. In Talmud Berachot 20a, we are told that women have the same obligation to pray as men, and that their prayers are equally accepted by God. The Mishnah in Berachot 20a and 20b informs us: "Women and servants and minors are exempt from recitation of Shema, and from wearing tefillin, and are obligated in prayer, in mezuzah and in grace after meals. (The reasons for the juxtaposition of women, servants, and minors will be discussed later on.)

In its analysis of the Mishnah, the Talmud concludes that the reason women are obligated in prayer is that prayer is a plea for mercy, and women, too, require mercy. So even though the verse in Psalms says one must pray evening, morning, and afternoon (thus making prayer a time-bound, positive commandment for which women are usually exempt) the Mishnah informs us that women *are* obligated in this particular instance.

Based on the Mishnah's proclamation, Rashi and Tosfot also agree that women, like men, are obligated to pray daily. As explained above, they hold that even though prayer is a time-bound, positive commandment, the special nature of prayer (the fact that it is a plea for mercy) outweighs "time" considerations. In addition to being a biblical commandment, they consider the obligation to pray daily to be a rabbinic law.

Ramban (Nachmanides), on the other hand, holds that the requirement for prayer is *only* a rabbinic enactment and not a biblical commandment. He writes in *Sefer Hamitzvot* positive commandment 5: "It is a privilege to pray and it is one of the merciful attributes of the Creator that He hears and responds whenever we call unto Him. The verse, 'And to serve Him with all your heart,' refers to worship in general, and not specifically to tefillah. It urges that our worship be sincere and wholeheartedly directed unto Him."

Nevertheless, Ramban conceded that in times of great distress the commandment of prayer is a biblical obligation. Such moments warrant our recognition that God is our only salvation. He continued to write, "It is a mitzvah to plead fervently with God through prayer and shofar blasts whenever the community is faced with great distress . . . for it is a mitzvah to affirm in moments of distress our belief that the Holy-One listens to prayers and intervenes to grant aid" (*Ibid.*). And so we learn that Ramban believed prayer to be biblically mandatory only when one is under duress. Otherwise, it is not to be considered an obligatory daily commandment. On the other hand, Rambam holds that the obligation to pray is a biblical one and that it is a positive commandment, though not time-bound. He believes we are biblically required to worship God at least once a day, with the time and text remaining open to personal choice. He goes on to say that it was the rabbis who introduced a fixed text and obligated us to pray at fixed times, twice daily. As he writes in *Hilchot Tefillah* 1:1–3: "The number of prayers that one recites every day is not of Torah origin. The setting of a definite time for prayer is not of Torah origin. Therefore, women are obligated in prayer, for it is a positive commandment which is not time-bound."

Both Rambam and Ramban regard prayer as meaningful only when derived from a sense of "צרה," distress, but they differ in their understanding of the word. Rambam regarded daily life itself to be difficult and full of moments of despair, hopelessness, absurdity, and lack of fulfillment. To him, an individual's daily life is a persistent "צרה." Ramban, however, regarded only public disasters and distresses as constituting "צרה."

Meiri to Berachot 20b writes that the rabbinic expansion of obligation of prayer applies to all those who were originally included in the biblical commandment. Since women were included in the biblical commandment, they are also included in the rabbinic expansion thereof. This statement applies, however, only to the morning and afternoon prayers, and not to the evening prayer. (Note: The evening prayer [*arbit*] was not originally considered obligatory by the rabbis—Talmud Berachot 27b.) Men have later come to accept it as an obligation, whereas women did not. Thus, women are not required to say the evening prayer.

Now to a discussion of the positioning of women with servants, and minors as quoted in the Mishnah Berachot 20a and 20b. (The quote, as cited earlier, reads: "Women and servants and minors are exempt from recitation of shema, and from wearing of tefillin, and are obligated in prayer, in mezuzah, and in grace after meals." This juxtaposition has often been pointed to by those unfamiliar with the general arrangement and rules that govern the learning of the Talmud as a justification for their claim that Judaism views women as inferior to men, and so places them in the same category as servants and minors. This point of view is definitely based upon misunderstanding and misinterpretation. The Talmud, as we know it today, was originally an oral tradition, which we received by word-of-mouth from Moses, our teacher, who in turn received it from the Holy-One-Blessed-be-He. It was only in the days of Rabbi Judah Ha-Nasi that the "Oral Tradition" was put in writing because circumstances of the time created the fear that it might otherwise be forgotten. Until then, Talmudic scholars were forced to commit large portions of the Oral Tradition to memory. And in order to make things easier to memorize, various means were employed. One method was to learn a law relating to a special situation by telling how it applied equally to a number of different types of people.

For instance, the law, "Everybody may slaughter, and his (or her) slaughtering is Kosher (ritually fit)" was followed with, "except that of a deaf person, a mentally ill person, and a minor" (Talmud Hulin 2a). "Women, and slaves, and minors are not counted toward a quorum for the grace after meals" (Talmud Berachot 45b). Other examples include: "Everybody is fit to read the Megillah, except a deaf person, a mentally ill person and a minor" (Talmud Megillah 19b). "Everybody is obligated to appear [at the Temple court on pilgrim Festivals of Passover, Pentecost, and Tabernacle], except a deaf person, a mentally ill person and a minor, a person of unknown sex, a hermaphrodite, women, unfreed slaves, the lame, the blind, the sick, the aged, and the one who is unable to go on foot" (Talmud Chagigah 2a). "Everybody is fit to bring [as a messenger] the bill of divorce, except a deaf person, a mentally ill person, and a minor, and a blind person, and a non-Jew" (Talmud Gittin 23a). And on and on. But we can learn from these few examples that the inclusion of women with slaves, minors, mentally retarded persons, etc., is not meant to equate, compare, or contrast them, but rather only to make it easier for the students of the Talmud to memorize the Mishnahs. The fact that women, at times, have a common halachic status with slaves, minors, etc., by no means implies that they have a common qualitative identity.

Yet another popular area of misconception and misinterpretation lies in the daily morning blessings, where every Jew thanks God for the different blessings He has bestowed upon him. One of the blessings that a man recites is: "Blessed are You God, the King of the Universe, who has not made me a woman." (This blessing is attributed to Rabbi Meir, Menahot 43b.) A woman says instead: "Blessed are You God, the King of the Universe, who has made me according to Your will." Or, in some versions, the general format "Blessed are You . . ." etc., is not mentioned but rather, "that you have made me according to Your will."

The commentary Amak Beracha, concurring with other authorities, states that the reason why men thank God for not making them women is because of men's fourteen extra opportunities (the time-bound, positive commandments) to perform the commandments of the Lord (from which women are exempted). Then he goes on to ask why women do not say, ". . . that You have made me a woman." His answer is because this would not show the superiority of

Jewish women (in terms of their obligation in commandments) over their non-Jewish counterparts (and female slaves) dwelling in the Land of Israel who are also obligated in the negative commandments and in the non-time-bound, positive ones. He continues that the women cannot say, ". . . that You have made me an Israelite woman," since the two preceding blessings would then seem to lose their purpose. (The two preceding blessings read, ". . . that You have not made me a gentile," and ". . . that You have not made me a slave." The term "Israelite woman," in itself, excludes being a slave or a non-Jew.) He therefore concludes that a woman says, ". . . that You have made me according to Your will," as meaning without obligation in certain of the positive commandments. Thus, in a way, a woman thanks God for making her close to His will, thereby making it *easier* for her to satisfy His will. Women, in this sense, are created closer to God's ideal of satisfaction.

Rabbi Samson Raphael Hirsch, in his commentary on the Siddur (prayer book), echoes this thought:[1] "And if our women have a smaller number of mitzvot (commandments) to fulfill than men, they know that the tasks which they must discharge as free Jewish women are no less in accordance with the will and desire of God than those of their brothers. Hence, their blessing is 'that created me according to His will.'"

The commentary on the Siddur, Mosah Davar, explains that man thanks God for not making him a woman because he feels he could not stand up to a woman's immense responsibilities, to the pain of childbirth and childbearing, to menstruation, and to the difficulties involved in raising children. As it is written: "I will greatly multiply your pain . . ." (Gen. 3:16).

---

[1] Rabbi Samson Raphael Hirsch, *Siddur* (Feldheim Publishers, New York, 1978), p. 13.

In today's world we find many women who peform very well at jobs previously held only by men. Men, on the other hand, are not generally able to perform as well when taking on responsibilities traditionally held by women. The tasks performed by women are far more difficult than those performed by men. Nevertheless, due to her superior virtues of modesty and humility, the woman accepts her lot gladly. She does not complain; instead she blesses the Lord who has made her according to His will.

A woman does not toil for the sake of reward, but rather to fulfill God's will. She thanks the Lord not for benefits (as does man, referring to the extra opportunities he has to perform *mitzvot*) but instead thanks Him for the toil itself. The woman thereby testifies that her toil is dearer to her than any benefits men receive. Eliyahu Kitov elucidates this point through the following example:[2]

> A king orders his army out to war. No man can say, "I do not want to go to war" or, "I want to go home from the front"; this is desertion. When a man returns home after the war the king rewards him. But no man can say I do not want any reward and I do not want to fight. If he says so he is a traitor—everyone must go to war when the king commands. There are times when a king asks for volunteers for a particularly difficult and dangerous task. The volunteers come forward and risk their lives to accomplish the task; the others watch them from afar with awe and fear. Those who did not volunteer bless the king for not having assigned the difficult task to them, which they would have never been able to perform. And the volunteers bless the king and thank him for having been chosen to do the task, in accordance to his will, and their will.

---

[2] A.E. Kitov, *The Jew and His Home* (Shengold Publishers Inc., 3rd Ed., New York, 1963), p. 69.

Women acknowledge their role differentiation (implicit in their exemption from certain commandments) by reciting their own blessing every morning. In so doing, they testify to and accept upon themselves God's overall plan for the world, the justification for which lies within the divine will and wisdom.

4
Women's Testimony

One of the commandments from which women are partially exempt is the obligation to bear witness. This positive commandment is derived from the following verse: "And if anyone sin in that he heard the voice of adjuration, he being a witness, whether he has seen or known, if he did not utter [it] then he shall bear his iniquity" (Lev. 5:1).

The Rambam (*Hilchot Edut* 9:1) enumerates ten different categories of people who are exempt from bearing witness. He cites two essential reasons for disqualification due to technical considerations and/or lack of credibility. For example, one who is blind in both eyes cannot be a witness since he does not fulfill the requirement of "... he has seen." Minors are not eligible as witnesses because the Torah states, "The two men between whom the controversy is shall stand before the Lord, before the priests and the judges that shall be in those days" (Deut. 19:17). "The two men" refers to "those of age," and not minors. The disqualification of relatives is derived from, "The fathers shall not be put to death for the children, neither shall the children be put to death for the fathers; every man shall be put to death for his own sin" (Deut. 24:16). Talmud Sanhedrin 27b concludes that the above verse refers to the testimony of fathers against sons, and vice versa. This is purely a technical rule based upon divine decree, not an assumption due to lack of credibility. The Rambam in *Hilchot Edut* 13:15 writes:

The disqualification of relatives by the Torah is not because it is assumed they love one another, for they cannot testify in favor of or against their relatives. It is merely a decree of the Torah. Therefore, a friend or enemy is qualified to testify, even though they are disqualified to judge the case. The Torah has only declared regarding the relatives.

A person is not qualified to testify against himself. The Rambam in Hilchot Sanhedrin 18:6 explains that this is due to both a technicality and because of lack of credibility. The insane and deaf mutes have no legal standing in Jewish courts. Their statements are totally unacceptable in a court of law both as litigants and as witnesses (see Talmud Shevuot 42a; Baba Batra 155b; Baba Kama 106b).

Non-Jews and slaves are technically ineligible to bear witness in a Jewish court of law. This law is derived from, "You shall do unto him as he had intended to do to his brother, so you shall put away the evil from your midst" (Deut. 19:19). ". . . to his brother . . ." refers to one who is obligated in the commandments, thus excluding non-Jews and servants.

We must keep in mind that with respect to obligation in the commandments, a woman is considered a fully obligated Jew. Her disqualification from testimony is also of a technical nature, however, and is derived from the following: לא יקום עד אחד באיש לכל־עון ולכל־חטאת בכל־חטא אשר יחטא על־פי שני עדים או על־פי שלשה עדים יקום דבר "One witness shall not rise up against a man for any iniquity, or for any sin, in any sin that he sins at the mouth of two witnesses or at the mouth of three witnesses shall a matter be established" (Deut. 19:15). In the Hebrew text, ". . . two witnesses . . ." appear in the male (and not female) gender, and thereby disqualify women from bearing witness (see Rambam *Hilchot Edut* 9:2). Additionally, in the Talmud Yerushalmi Yoma 6:1, the rabbis learn by method of exegetical analysis that women, slaves, and minors may not testify.

Women are only partially disqualified from testifying, however. There are a number of instances where women can bear witnesses, as explained by Rashba (*Shaalot U'Teshubot ha-Rashba ha-meyuhasot le'ha-Ramban,* No. 74):

> Whenever the rabbis merely required ascertainmentt of truth, they did not distinguish between one witness or two. Thus, in a case of ascertaining whether a woman's husband is alive or dead, where we are concerned only with credibility, we may accept the testimony of all those who are technically disqualified, even one woman is acceptable. Since it is only where witnessed testimony is required that one requires two witnesses free from all technical disqualifications.

In ritual matters, credible statements, rather than witnessed testimony, are required. Thus the statements of men or women pertaining to areas such as Kashrut and Family Purity are equally acceptable.

The Jewish criminal justice system stands unique among nations. According to Jewish law, knowledge beyond the shadow of a doubt is not in and of itself sufficient evidence for conviction. Requirements of credibility of witnesses is but one of several such specified requirements, in addition to the many technical conditions necessary for witnessed testimony. The following excerpt from the Talmud Shevuot 34a illustrates this point:

> We have learned that Rabbi Shimon ben Shetah said, "I once saw a man running after his friend into a desert area and I ran after him and found a sword in his hand and blood dripping and a man killed, and I said: 'Evil man, who killed this man, either you or I, but what can I do, for your life is not given into my hands, for the Torah said, "According to the statement of two or three witnesses shall the convicted one die" (Deut. 17:6), but the Almighty will punish you.'" Before Rabbi Shimon left, a snake came and bit the man and he died.

Hence, even if two men see two people enter a room and then they find one man dead and the other holding a knife in his hand, the two men do not qualify as valid witnesses to testify against the presumed murderer.

Besides the technical requirement of two valid witnesses, Jewish law specifies that the two witnesses must see each other, as well as the person committing the crime. If they did not see each other, their testimony still holds full credibility, but it cannot be used for conviction. In addition, there are many technical requirements for bearing witness, most of which demonstrate that knowledge beyond the shadow of a doubt is not enough to convict the accused. Hence, when witnessed testimony is required, i.e. for the purpose of accusations, two witnesses free from all technical disqualifications are necessary, and women will not do.

Nevertheless, Jewish women possess full credibility. The following illustrates this point. If two litigants come to court with inadequate evidence on either side, one way to assess the facts in such a situation is to administer an oath to one of the parties; either to the plaintiff or the defendant, depending on specific laws set down for the particular case. There are a number of people who are ineligible to take an oath. These include slaves, deaf mutes, insane persons, minors, etc.—but not women. Because in Jewish law an oath is only administered to persons with credibility, we learn that as far as the Jewish law is concerned, both men and women are equally credible.

And this concept of equal credibility can be utilized by courts to make judgements. As the Rambam writes in *Hilchot Sanhedrin* 24:1:

> A judge may decide monetary cases on the basis of matters that impress him as true and he is totally convinced that the matter is so. In this case he may judge according to what he knows . . . even if the witness is a woman . . . as long as they have credibility with him and the case impresses him as correct and strong, he may rely on it and judge . . . If it is so, why did the Torah

require two witnesses? For where two witnesses come in front of the judge, he may judge on their testimony, even though he does not know whether they told the truth or lied.

So here the Rambam, too, clearly subscribes to the notion that women are credible.

Rama in *Hoshen Mishpat* 35:14 further amplifies this point:

> There are those who say that earlier generations have enacted that we accept the testimony of women in regard to those (financial) cases where male witnesses are not readily available. Such instances occur when a case arises regarding a matter in the woman's section of the synagogue or in other occasions where a woman happens to be present and there is no man. Consequently, some have written that even one woman is to be believed in the cases of personal injury, etc. . . . The rationale being that the plaintiff cannot arrange to have male witnesses present.

So why are women technically disqualified to testify in certain areas of witnessed testimony? Like many other aspects of Jewish law, this might be understood, simply, as a heavenly decree or it might be looked at as having deeper implications.

A king is disqualified from being a witness (see Rambam, *Hilchot Melachim* 3:7). Illustrious kings of Israel—even David and Solomon—could not testify; the reason being that the attitude of the court to a witness and the respect due a king are contradictory. In a similar vein, it would be contradictory to the basic principles of the private role of women in Jewish life to require them to testify at all times (as has been stated, "The entire glory of the daughter of a king lies on the inside"). Women, therefore, are even exempt from the requirement that a litigant must appear himself in a court, rather than appoint an attorney to appear in his stead (Talmud Shevuot 30a and the Tosfot there; Gittin 41a; Ketubot 74b). The rabbis also felt it would be improper to subject women to the undignified, intense, and aggressive cross-examination that normally occurs in the courtroom.

Thus, we learn women are disqualified from the obligation to testify only where witnessed testimony is required, and that is purely for technical reasons. Women retain equal credibility with men; their oath is fully acceptable in court, as is the oath of any credible individual.

5
Women, Marriage, and Divorce

Marriage is one of the most sacred institutions of Judaism. According to our sages, there are three basic purposes for marriage: (1) to beget children; (2) to avoid illicit sexual relations; and (3) to provide each person with the opportunity to become a complete functioning unit. Rambam in *Hilchot Ishut* 1:2 describes the commandment to acquire a wife as a positive commandment incumbent upon the man. "And their [meaning "women"] acquisition is a positive Torah commandment, and they are acquired by one of these three means: by money, by contract, or by cohabitation. Cohabitation and contract are from the Torah, and money through [the institution of] the rabbis . . ."

The word "acquisition" קנין in Hebrew, does not refer simply to financial ownership, but rather connotes a change in status. Thus, in Jewish law, there are two kinds of contracts: the קנין איסור, a contract which essentially effects a change in personal or ritual status, and the קנין ממון, a contract which essentially effects a monetary change. The word קנין can also be understood through its metaphoric use in biblical and rabbinic literature to indicate an establishment of a close and intimate relationship.

As it relates to marriage, the word קנין connotes both the establishment of a close, intimate relationship and a contract which results in a change of ritual status.

The use of the word קנין, "acquisition," in this context has led many to believe that women are considered acquired objects. But such is not the case. According to Jewish law, a contract is written by the one who receives the money—not by the purchaser, but by the seller. When it comes to marriage, we find it is the *man* and not the woman who writes the contract (see Talmud Kiddushin 5a). Therefore, according to many halachic authorities, the wife is never considered the husband's property. And a husband is not permitted to restrict his wife's freedom of movement, ". . . for she is not in jail where she may not come and go . . ." (Rambam, *Hilchot Ishut* 13:11). Thus, the word קנין, as it pertains to marriage, does not mean "purchase" but rather delineates a ritual change in status, and the establishment of a close, intimate relationship between husband and wife.

Although the Torah bids man to actively seek a wife, marriage is a contract created by the willing consent of both parties. As to why *man,* and not *woman,* is commanded to seek a mate, one might explain that since woman was created from part of the man's body, it would be natural for the one who has lost something to search for it and seek to be reunited with it (see Talmud Niddah 31b). Another possible reason lies in women's (in general) inherent desire to have a family. Thus the Bible did not deem it necessary to command them to seek such fulfillment. However men, in general, might be less inclined to form a family and so gain the extra responsibilities of wife and children. Also, as men get involved with advancing their careers, they may forget or not wish to make time for family matters. For all the above reasons, it was felt necessary to specifically command the man to seek a wife.

The rabbis have enacted several edicts to ensure justice and fairness toward women in matters of marriage. According to Torah law, a man may marry a woman by authorizing another person to engage her by the prescribed legal ceremony to be his wife. But Rab, a well respected Talmudic authority, forbade such marriage by proxy. He reasoned that when the man meets his wife, he might find in her some displeasing traits and dislike her (see Kiddushin 41a). In a similar ruling, Rab forbade the marriage of minors. The Torah originally authorized a father to marry off his minor daughter to whomever he pleased. The rabbis, however, forbade this practice and ruled that a father may marry off a minor only if she explicitly agrees to marry the person of her own free will (Ibid).

To further protect the wife, the rabbis introduced in the marriage contract (*ketubah*) an obligation upon the husband to pay his wife a specified sum of money in the event of divorce. The husband was also obligated to pay for his wife's medical treatment in case she became ill, to pay her ransom should she be kidnapped, to pay for all her burial expenses, and to arrange for her maintenance through his estates for as long as she remained a widow (Rambam, *Hilchot Ishut* 12:2).

So we see that in addition to the threefold biblical obligation of the husband toward his wife—i.e., to provide her with food and clothing and to respect her conjugal rights—the rabbis introduced many other duties upon the husband which would strengthen the status of the married woman.

The Torah realizes that not all marriages can be successful, and there are times when a marriage should be dissolved. At such times, the man is commanded to divorce his wife (see Deut. 24:1-3). Divorce, like marriage, is a unilateral contract. According to the Bible, the laws of divorce empower the man to divorce his wife and not vice versa. Also, a man cannot be compelled to divorce his wife, but may do so only of his own free will. One may ask—why is it that only the man can divorce his wife? Critics—who may wish to answer this question by claiming it is another instance where Jewish law acknowledges male dominance—will find their claim doubtful, to say the least. We need only look at the rather puzzling difference in Jewish law between what is considered a divorce for Jewish couples and divorce for non-Jewish couples. The Midrash Genesis Rabbah 18:8 offers three opinions on the topic of divorce for non-Jews: (1) divorce is exclusively dependent on the wife; (2) divorce may depend on either half of the couples; and (3) divorce is impossible. However, Rambam in *Hilchot Melachim* 9:8 writes:

> And from when will the wife of his friend be considered as a divorcee? From the time he sends her from his house or when she leaves his house and goes out on her own. Since non-Jews do not have a bill of divorce and it does not depend on him alone, but anytime he or she wants to leave the other, they are divorced.

Unfortunately, a number of unscrupulous men did take advantage of our rather lenient laws of divorce. Because they did not live up to Torah standards of justice, fairness, and fear of God, the rabbis found it necessary to institute specific enactments to protect women's rights.

For instance, the *ketubah* (Jewish marriage contract) obligates a man who divorces his wife to pay her a statutory minimum lump sum equivalent to one year's support, and to support her with alimony payments thereafter. The rabbis realized that a man who cannot afford the stiff payments of the *ketubah* may decide to use any perverse and corrupt means available to agonize and terrorize his wife by refusing to grant her a divorce when one is in order. Therefore, the rabbis empowered the Jewish courts of law to review claims made by women against their husbands. If such claims were found to constitute valid reasons for divorce, the Jewish court can and will order the husband to divorce his wife, and the court may use all its powers to force him to do so. In this way, the rabbis insured that women are never left completely at their husband's mercy.

Rambam in *Hilchot Gerushin* 2:20 writes:

Whenever the law requires that a husband be ordered to divorce his wife and he refuses to do so, the Jewish court of law at any place and at any time may impose corporal punishment on him until he says: "I am willing, and the divorce bill is valid." Similarly, if the non-Jewish court beat him and told him: "Do what the Jewish court instructs you," and the Jewish court pressured him through the non-Jewish court until he executed a Jewish divorce, it is a valid divorce. If the non-Jewish court, on its own, forced him to write the bill of divorce, since one is required, it is valid according to Torah law, but was disqualified by rabbinic enactment (so that the women should approach the Jewish court first).

Therefore, although a woman may approach the Jewish court to force her husband to grant her a divorce, she may not initially approach a non-Jewish court to do so. However, if a Jewish court orders a Jewish divorce and the non-Jewish court merely enforces the decision of the Jewish court, the divorce is valid.

In Mishnah Ketubot 7:10 we learn, "These are the husbands whom one [Jewish court] compels to divorce their wives: a person with severe boils, a person suffering from a bad odor from the nose, the worker whose job entails collecting excrement of dogs, a copper miner, and a tanner."

Except for the first item, in all these cases the common reason for granting a divorce is the husband's repulsive bodily odor. So we see it was assumed one cannot force a wife to continue living with her husband under such distasteful circumstances.

According to Rabbi Meir, the wife may insist upon a divorce even if she knew prior to the marriage of her husband's physical condition or type of work and had willingly agreed to marry him nonetheless. The woman is entitled to change her mind. She may claim before the court, "I thought I could withstand it, but now I see that I cannot." The majority of rabbis, however, do not agree with Rabbi Meir's opinion.

There are a number of other instances where the husband is urged and, if necessary, forced to divorce his wife. From Shulchan Aruch, Even Ha-Ezer 77:1 we learn:

> A husband who rebels against his wife and says: "I will provide for her maintenance, but I refuse conjugal relationship with her because I hate her," then [initially] one adds weekly . . . to her ketuba [to the sum of money the husband has to pay her in case of divorce] and lets her dwell with him so long as she desires. But even though the value of her ketuba increases continually, the husband transgresses a biblical commandment [by denying her conjugal rights] . . . However, if she wishes, one forces him immediately [to divorce her].

On the other hand, if the wife refuses conjugal relations with her husband, she is called a rebellious wife and her husband may be compelled to divorce her. As Rambam writes in *Hilchot Ishut* 14:8:

> A woman who refuses conjugal relationship with her husband is called "rebellious." One has to ask her why she rebels. If she says: "I hate him and cannot have intercourse with him," one compels her husband to divorce her. For she is not like a captive woman that she should submit to one she hates and she forfeits her ketubah.

A number of halachic authorities disagree with Rambam's view. They argue that in a case where the wife sets her eyes on another man, she could simply claim she cannot endure her husband and thus receive a divorce. A compromise view is suggested by Rav in Tosfos R'Y'D Ketubot 63a:

> If she says that she hates him, one does not force her to stay with him by warning her with the loss of the value of her ketubah. One lets her remain in her attitude (towards her husband). Since her husband is displeasing to her, it is as if she is coerced in the matter. She cannot help herself. Even a pious and upright woman cannot submit to a husband whom she rejects . . . even

if one is unable to notice any blemishes in him. These things happen quite often. This is not like the case of a person who is unable to eat a certain kind of food that is detestable to him. There is no way here to coerce her. One should rather intercede with her, to influence her to accept him. Moreover, if we were sure that what she says was true, that he is indeed repulsive to her and she did not just "set her eyes on another man," we would compel the husband to divorce her as in the other cases in the Mishnah of "And these are the husbands whom we force to divorce her . . ." for similar reasons . . . In this case, we happen to doubt the honesty of her statement, because we do not find in her husband those blemishes that she asserts . . . Therefore, we cannot compel the husband to divorce her; but we do not punish her with the loss of the monetary value of her ketubah. Maybe she does speak the truth, for (it is written) "The heart knows its own bitterness" (Proverbs 14:10).

In all, if the Jewish court of law finds merit to the claims of a wife against her husband, it may force the husband to grant her a divorce.

The rabbis introduced a number of innovative enactments to further protect the rights of the married woman. A major concern is to protect the wife against becoming an *agunah*; a woman whose husband, for whatever reasons, is not available to give her a divorce. Legally, an *agunah* is considered married, and even though she has no husband, she cannot remarry. In order to reduce the likelihood of this happening, the rabbis applied more lenient rules toward conditions for an acceptable and legally valid divorce. For example, when a messenger brought a bill of divorce (sent by a husband to his wife) from Babylon to the land of Israel, the messenger was required to testify that the bill was written according to the Torah requirements; i.e. in his name and in her name and for the purposes of divorce. Even though under normal circumstances two witnesses are required to testify, the rabbis declared that the testimony of the messenger alone was sufficient. In a case where the parties were separated by great distances, the rabbis knew that if they were to insist on two witnesses, prolonged delays could occur in the sending of a divorce bill or, even worse, it might never be sent at all. This would leave the woman in the terrible state of being an agunah (see Talmud Gittin 3a). Thus, if the husband went to a faraway country with which there was no possibility of normal communication, the rabbis accepted the testimony of one witness arrived from that land. In such cases, they even went so far as accepting the testimony of the wife herself. Here even the testimony of slaves are admissable. Also, normally, according to Torah law, one may testify from direct personal knowledge but not on the basis of information gathered from another person's testimony. In the case of a long-distance divorce, however, the witness is allowed to testify on the basis of testimony he heard from another source.

In Talmud Gittin 19b we learn of another enactment to prevent a woman from becoming an agunah. Normally, a bill of divorce requires the signature of two witnesses. But if the witnesses were unable to sign their names, the rabbis allowed them to merely fill in with ink their prefigured signatures on the bill.

Levirate marriage is another area of marriage and divorce which may be troublesome and problematic for women. According to the Torah, if a man dies without leaving any offspring, one of his brothers is required to marry his widow (see Deut. 25:5). But what if the widow and her brother-in-law are not suited for one another . . . or she simply has no desire to marry him? In Talmud Yebamot 44a and 106a we find that if the age difference is too great, if she is very old and he is very young or vice versa, he is told, "Why would you want to marry somebody so much younger or older than you, go find someone like yourself and avoid quarrel in your house." This is in accordance with the biblical verse, "The elders of his city shall call him and speak to him . . ." (Deut. 25:8).

In the case of an unfitting brother-in-law, one must urge *halitzah*, the ceremony by which the wife will be free by Jewish law to marry somebody other than her dead husband's brother. In Mishnah Ketubot 7:10 we reviewed situations where a wife may seek a divorce from her husband. For example, if her dead husband was a tanner and her brother-in-law is also a tanner, she may refuse to marry the brother-in-law, claiming, "I was willing to accept your brother, but I cannot accept you." In this case the rabbis would urge and approve of *halitzah*. Another instance would be if it were known that the brother-in-law intended to marry his sister-in-law merely to acquire her wealth. The rabbis did not compel him to free her by halitzah, but did try to mislead him. It was permissible, for example, to promise him a sum of money if he agreed to halitzah and then not pay up after the ceremony. Thus we learn that even if the halitzah ceremony was executed under false assumptions on the part of the brother-in-law, it is nonetheless valid (see Talmud Yebamot 106a).

Despite all the attempts by our rabbis to protect women's rights and privileges in matters of marriage and divorce, there still occur some unfortunate instances where—technically and legally—not much can be done. These unfortunate situations are left to be dealt with in the following ways. In the case where a husband abuses the technical legalities of the Jewish law and does not act in accordance with the spirit of the law, one is reminded of one of the most powerful principles in Judaism. "By the same measure that one treats others he will be treated" (Talmud Sotah 8b). This is one of the cardinal laws of divine retribution or reward which spares no one (see Talmud Sanhedrin 90a). In the case where a wife is oppressed or remains an *agunah*, one may say that it is the divine will, for whatever reasons He deemed fit. It is similar to when a man finds himself oppressed by illness or other unfortunate happenings in the physical world, and must realize the hand of God. However, just as acceptance of disease as part of the divine scheme does not preclude seeking treatment, so, too, the acceptance of moral injustice and oppression as divine will does not preclude seeking all possible means to fight it (see Talmud Baba Metziah 38b).

Proponents of Jewish law have formed numerous enactments to protect the wife's rights and privileges in the area of marriage and divorce. The rabbis always have and always will show a willingness and readiness to do everything possible to ensure justice and fairness in this highly sensitive and supremely important area of Jewish life.

Part Four

THE KEY TO THE CONTINUAL SURVIVAL OF THE JEWS

I
Jews and Morality

Jews are well known for their practice of principles of morality. Morality has always been one of our most basic sustainers; it is the key to our survival. The Jewish nation cannot survive without strict adherence to the laws of morality given to us by the Holy-One-Blessed-be-He. So much so, that the existence of the Jewish nation has been seriously threatened whenever one of the fundamental laws of morality has been infringed upon.

The three fundamental laws of morality are also three of the Ten Commandments. They are: (1) The prohibition (and severe denouncement) of idol worship. (2) The (strict) prohibition against murder. (3) The (strict) prohibition against adultery. These laws are so crucial that a Jew is obligated to martyr himself rather than commit any of the above offenses. (See Talmud Sanhedrin 74a.)

In general, a Jew is commanded to observe God's commandments so that "he live by them" (Lev. 18:5). From this our rabbis learn that if, for example, a person is sick and will only recover by eating pork or another non-kosher food, then the sick person is not only allowed but *obligated* to eat the non-kosher food, so that he may live. Similar allowances and obligations apply to all of the 613 commandments except for the three particular commandments mentioned above. The reason for these three exceptions is that these commandments are so essential to our survival as individuals and as a nation that they cannot be overlooked under any circumstances, and the principle of "to live by them" does not apply.

According to Targum Yonaton, the punishment for immorality is a plague that ravishes the world, destroying the righteous and the wicked alike. Rashi echoes this opinion while commenting on Genesis 7:13: "The end of all flesh has come before Me; for the earth is filled with violence through them; and behold I will destroy them." Here God is informing Noah of His intention to destroy the world and explains His reason for doing so. Rashi comments that wherever you find immorality and idol worship, indiscriminate punishment—regardless of guilt or innocence—comes upon the world, killing good and bad alike.

We see, therefore, that the very existence of the Jewish people (and human beings in general) is dependent on the observance of these three fundamental laws. The following further amplifies this point:

While in the desert and waiting for Moses to give them the Torah, the children of Israel miscalculated the time Moses would spend on Mount Sinai and thought his delay meant he would not be coming back. So they made an idol, the golden calf, and began to worship it. God's anger was kindled, as it says in the Bible: "And My wrath may wax hot against them that I may devour them" (Exod. 32:10). After Moses interceded, God forgave the nation as a whole. However, those who sinned against Him by worshipping the golden calf were put to death.

In Leviticus chapter 20, while admonishing against a particular type of idol worship, God says: "I will set My face against that man and will cut him off from among his people" (Lev. 20:3). According to Rashi, this means God will turn aside from all his pursuits in order to punish the person who has been engaged in idol worship.

In parshat Shema, Deuteronomy chapter 11, the Jewish nation as a whole is warned against idolatry. The Torah threatens: "And anger of the Lord be kindled against you, and He shall shut up the heaven, so that there shall be no rain, and the ground shall not yield her fruit, and you shall quickly perish from off the good land which the Lord gives you" (Deut. 11:17). It is obvious: idol worship can bring about total annihilation of the Jewish people.

Murder is a terrible crime. We are all created in the image of God, and if one murders a human being, it is as if one denies the existence of God. Our Sages said that one who saves a life is considerd to have saved the entire world. On the other hand, one who takes a live is considered to have destroyed the entire world.

In Deuteronomy chapter 21, the Torah presents special laws concerning the victim of a slaying whose murderer(s) is (are) not known. First, the Torah commands that the elders of the city (i.e., the members of the Great Sanhedrin, Rashi quoting Sotah 44a) and the judges determine the exact place where the body was found and its proximity to the nearest city. Then, "The elders of that city shall bring down the heifer unto a rough valley, which may neither be plowed nor sown, and shall break the heifer's neck there in the valley" (Deut. 21:4), and then the elders ". . . shall wash their hands over the heifer whose neck was broken in the valley" (Deut. 21:6). Afterwards, the priests say: "Forgive Your people Israel, whom You have redeemed, O' Lord, and suffer not innocent blood to remain in the midst of Your people Israel, and blood shall be forgiven to them" (Deut. 21:8) (Rambam, *Hilchot Rotziach ve-Shemirat Nefesh* ch. 9, Sanhedrin 14a), and thus they make atonement for the children of Israel. We see, then, that murder is a terrible crime with terrible consequences for the Jewish people if it is not prevented or atoned for.

Adultery is another terrible crime. The very word, תנאף (*tin-af*), adultery, is a contraction of two words: תן אף (*ten and af*) which means "give anger." It alludes to the enormity of the sin and its dire consequences in kindling the wrath of

God. God assures swift judgment to adulterers and sorcerers in Malachi 3:5: "And I (God) will come near to you to [hold] judgment, and I will be a swift witness against the sorcerers and against adulterers."

A terrible tragedy in our history is recorded in the Book of Judges chapter 19. On a journey to the House of the Lord, a man and his concubine came to the city of Gibeah, which belonged to the tribe of Benjamin. Upon the insistence of an old, good-hearted man, they took lodging in his house. Shortly afterwards, the wicked people of the city surrounded the house, and began beating at the door. After a brief conversation with the wicked men who wanted to have homosexual relations with the guest, the guest, wanting to save himself from this most abominable abuse, grabbed his concubine and brought her forth to the men outside. The wicked men of the city then grabbed the concubine and had relations with her the entire night until morning. In the morning, the man found his concubine dead at the entrance of the house. The man returned to his hometown and spread the news of the atrocity of the wicked men of Gibeah throughout all the tribes of Israel. The children of Israel were enormously troubled by this terrible crime and assembled in order to make amends for it. They sent messengers to the tribe of Benjamin, asking them to surrender the perpetrators of this heinous act. Upon the refusal of the tribe of Benjamin to cooperate in executing justice, the rest of the tribes of Israel asked God whether to go up against the criminals and wage war against the tribe of Benjamin. God answered: "Go up, for tomorrow I will deliver them into your hand" (Judges 20:28). After a number of fierce battles, in which a substantial number of Benjaminites were killed, the tribes executed justice, thereby preventing the wrath of God from turning against all of Israel.

After Balaam's effort upon the request of Balak (the king of the Moabites) to curse the children of Israel failed, Balaam said to Balak: "Come, I will advise you what this people shall do to your people in the end of the days" (Num. 24:14). Rashi quoting the Talmud Sanhedrin 106a comments that Balaam's advice was as follows: The God of these people is a Hater of harlotry; therefore, the choice means of destroying them is by causing them to stumble through harlotry. So they conspired, ". . . and the people (Israelites) began to commit harlotry with the daughters of Moab. And they called the people unto the sacrifices of their gods; and the people did eat and bowed down to their gods. And Israel joined itself unto *Baal* of *Peor* (an idol), and the anger of the Lord was kindled against Israel" (Num. 25:1-3).

Immediately thereafter, a plague befell the children of Israel. And God commanded the chiefs of the people to try those engaged in idolatry and hang them if convicted (Talmud Sanhedrin 35a), ". . . so that the fierce anger of the Lord may turn away from Israel" (Num. 25:4). Later, in Deuteronomy 4:3-4, Moses admonished the children of Israel: "Your eyes have seen what the Lord did in *Baal-Peor* for all the men that followed after the *Baal* of *Peor*, the Lord has destroyed them from the midst of you. And you that cleave to the Lord your God are alive everyone of you this day."

In the two tablets on which the ten commandments are written, the commandment against idol worship, on the one tablet, appears directly opposite the commandment against adultery, on the other. This opposition alludes to the fact that someone who betrays his spouse will betray God Himself (Mechilta).

Prophets who admonished Israel against idol worship often compared the unfaithful nation to a harlot and an adulterous wife. (The Jewish nation is compared to a bride, God is compared to a groom, and the Torah is the marriage contract given to God's bride, Israel.) "Thus said the Lord Eternal, whereas your wealth was squandered, and your nakedness was uncovered through your lewd acts with your lovers, and with all your abominable idols, and for the blood of your children, whom you did give to them. Therefore, behold I will gather all your lovers, whom you have given pleasure, and all whom you have loved together with all of whom you have hated, yea, I will gather them all about you and will uncover your nakedness. And I will judge you, as adulteresses and women that shed blood are judged, and I will bring upon you the blood of fury and jealousy" (Ezekiel 17:36-38).

Throughout the Torah, there are clear references to the special relationship between God and His nation Israel. "For you are a holy people unto the Lord your God, and the Lord has chosen you to be a people of select portion unto Himself out of all peoples that are upon the face of the earth" (Deut. 14:2). "And you shall be holy unto Me, for I the Lord am Holy and have set you apart from the peoples that you should be mine" (Lev. 20:26).

We are repeatedly reminded that we are the chosen people of the Lord and that we should be holy. How is this holiness achieved? The Torah answers: "You shall keep all My statutes, and all My ordinances, and do them, that the land whither I bring you not vomit you out. And you shall not walk in the customs of the nation which I am casting out before you, for all these things they did, and I abhored them" (Lev. 20:22-23). From this we learn that holiness is achieved by separating the Jewish nation from the perverted and futile values of its surrounding cultures. Holiness is also achieved through observing God's commandments, and especially by staying away from immoralities. Leviticus 19:2 says: "You shall be holy, because I the Lord your God am holy;" to which Rashi comments: "Separate yourself from incest and from transgression, for wherever you find a fence around incest you find (mention of) holiness."

Let us now take a sociological and psychological look at the issue of morality in the context of the three fundamental commandments discussed earlier.

If you were to establish a community, how would you ensure its well-being and continued survival? First, you would probably decide on some rules and regulations to attain such goals. More importantly, you would set up an authority with the power to mete out punishment who would serve as a deterrent against infractions of the laws and regulations that were set up for the welfare of your community. Can you imagine what a community would be like without laws and regulations and an authority to enforce them? Everybody could go around and kill people or commit adultery at will. If the intelligence of man was employed to do evil, your community would be worse than a chaotic jungle. It would not take long before the whole community was destroyed through violence due to lack of any fear of retribution. Therefore, Rabbi Chanina said, "Pray for the welfare of the government, since but for the fear thereof, men would swallow each other alive" (Mishnah Abot 3:2).

The ultimate authority in the community of the world is the Almighty. Fear of His retribution fills our hearts; on the other hand, we know that He is a benevolent authority who wants only what is best for us. Among all the rules and laws that He gave us, there are three fundamental rules upon which our existence depends: first, to recognize Him by not worshipping idols; and second and third, not to destroy His world by involving ourselves in murder and in adultery.

The Creator was and is well aware of our needs. He knows that every human being has a tendency, an inclination, to do evil (the Evil Inclination). In fact, the Bible itself testifies to this assertion: "For the imagination of the heart of man [is] evil from his youth" (Gen. 8:21). Rashi comments that from the time the embryo bestirs itself to come out from its mother's womb, the Evil Inclination is placed in it. Similarly, we find in Genesis 4:7 "... Sin croucheth at the door..." That is, the Evil Inclination is always ready and waiting nearby to induce us to sin. And in Deuteronomy 31:21, God says: "For I [God] know their inclination [of the children of Israel]." And the Psalmist informs us, "God knows the thoughts of man, that they are futile" (Ps. 94:11).

Furthermore, we are commanded in parshat Shema: "And you shall love the Lord your God with all your heart and with all your soul and with all your might" (Deut. 6:5). Rashi quotes Siphre (also found in Talmud Berachot 54a) and explains that "with all your heart" means with both your inclinations—the Evil and the Good Inclinations—which exist within all of us.

It is well known that when man is asked to do something or warned not to do something, the Evil Inclination urges him to disobey the command. (Incidentally, this imposed extra difficulty is why a woman who fulfills a time-bound, positive commandment for which she has no obligation receives less of a reward than a man for fulfilling the same commandment. Because men *are* obligated, the commandment becomes harder for them to fulfill.)

Even the most righteous Jew is prone to be induced by the Evil Inclination to disobey the Lord; nobody is immune from this tendency. Even our righteous King David yielded to His Evil Inclination and sinned against God by having intimate relations with Bath Sheva, who was not his wife at that time. And he later testified to this Evil Inclination in Psalms 103:14 "For He knows our inclination."

The wisest of all men, King Solomon himself, was also a victim of his Evil Inclination. He, too, sinned against the Lord, and he, too, testified to man's imperfection and inclination to sin. King Solomon said: "No man on earth is so wholly righteous that he always does good and never sins" (Ecclesiastes 7:20).

It is obvious we could all use some sort of protection against this powerful Evil Inclination. For this reason, the Torah was given to us—in order to teach us how to modify our behavior, rather than allow instinctual urges to rule our every move. Many of the laws in Judaism that permeate our daily lives and activities are meant to safeguard us against the Evil Inclination. As such, the Jewish religion is a staunch advocate of preventive medicine. Our preventive medicine is our Torah, and our rich tradition. Our doctors (our rabbis), under the direction of our Chief Physician (our God and His everlasting Torah), have formulated a prescription of preventive medication (the detailed laws of the Bible and Talmud) to protect us against any spiritual malaise which could eventually lead to physical malaise and our own destruction. The following discussion of *mechitzah,* the physical separation between men and women in the synagogue, illustrates this idea.

2
Mechitzah

Prayer constitutes one of the central activities of our lives as Jews. By serving as a direct link between us and our Creator and Sustainer, it provides a unique opportunity for every Jew to address God personally, ask Him to fulfill his needs, and thank Him for all He has done. Rabbi Joseph Soloveitchik depicts the ideal arrangement for prayer:[1]

> Prayer means communication with the Master of the World, and therefore withdrawal from all and everything. During prayer man must feel alone, removed, isolated. He must then regard the Creator as an only Friend, from whom alone he can hope for support and consolation. "Behold, as the eyes of servants look unto the hand of their master, as the eyes of a maiden unto the hand of her mistress; so our eyes look unto the Lord our God, until He be gracious to us" (Ps. 123:2).
>
> Clearly, the presence of women among men, or of men among women, which often evokes certain frivolity in the group, either in spirit or in behavior, can contribute little to sanctification or to the deepening of religious feeling; nor can it help instill that mood in which a man must be immersed when he would communicate with the Almighty. "Out of the depth have I called thee, O Lord" (Ps. 130:1), says the Psalmist.

The existence of *mechitzah,* a physical separation between men and women in the synagogue, is a biblical injunction.

---

[1] Baruch Litvin, *The Sanctity of Synagogue* (Spero Foundation, New York, 1959) p. 116.

The Talmud Succah 51 a,b discusses the balcony that was erected in the women's court of the Temple for the eve of the second day of the Feast of Tabernacles, so that women—in the upper level—and men—in the lower level—could watch the Simchat Beth ha-Shoebah, the festivity of drawing water for libation. But where lies the biblical injunction? Our Sages understood this biblical injunction from Zechariah 12:12-14: "And the land will mourn, every family apart by itself, the family of the House of David apart, and their wives apart. The family of the House of Levi apart, and their wives apart, the family of the House of Shimi apart, and their wives apart. All the families that remain, every family apart by itself, and their wives apart." The Talmud Succah 52a derives from the above that if in a situation of sadness such as mourning, when the Evil Inclination is not so strong, men and women are required to be separate, how much more so should they be separated at a time of joy, when the Evil Inclination is much stronger.

But what is the underlying function of a mechitzah? It is obvious that at the festivity of drawing water there was not the fear that a man and a woman would seclude themselves (a situation clearly forbidden by the Jewish law) since so many men and women were present, and since the two passageways remained open (with people constantly passing through—to leave through the Temple mount, the rampart enclosure, the women's court, the general courtyard, and hence outside). Rather, the fear was only that of the onset of a frivolous mood. In fact, originally in the women's court of the Temple, women were within and men, outside. Rashi explains that women were actually in the women's court proper, and men were in the Temple mount and the enclosure within the rampart, with a great *mechitzah* between them. However, since people had to stand near the open gate to see the proceedings, it was noticed that levity soon set in. The Sages then decided to reverse the arrangement, putting the women outside and the men inside. But this new arrangement proved to be inadequate too. As the *mechitzah* did not fully separate men and women from each other's view (they could still see right through the open gates), levity still persisted. Then the ideal solution was found. By constructing a balcony and placing women above and men below, there would be no chance of mingling or communication between the sexes and so no onset of frivolity.

Since the destruction of the Temple, we offer our prayers (symbolizing the offerings that used to be brought to the Holy Temple), in our sanctuaries-in-miniature, our synagogues. "Therefore say: Thus says my Lord God, though I have removed them far off among the nations, and though I have scattered them among the countries, yet I have been for them a small sanctuary [Targum translates this as 'synagogue'] in the countries where they came" (Yechezkel 11:16). The laws of *mechitzah,* therefore, apply equally to these sanctuaries-in-miniature; and the mingling of the sexes is proscribed (Megillah 29a, Tur and Shulchan Aruch Orah Hachaim 151). In fact, these laws apply to any occasion where the gathering of men and women might lead to frivolity. Rabbi Moshe Feinstein[2] elaborates on these points:

> It might be argued, however, that only in the Temple was such separation required by biblical law, because of the injunction in the verse, "My sanctuary ye shall reverence" (Lev. 19:30, 26:2), for if one is frivolous he is certainly not reverent; hence, it may be argued, in the synagogue this law may obtain only because the Sages extended the ban against levity to synagogue. . . . And yet, during the prayer the Name of Heaven and matters of Torah and holiness are mentioned, it is therefore reasonable to assume that the injunction here is biblical too. Indeed, R. Nissim in his Novellae to Megillah, folio 26, writes that kedushah, the doxology of sanctification, was instituted in synagogue prayer, because in essence the synagogue was designed to recite therein matters of holiness. Now if these "matters of holiness" are themselves not recited under conditions of sanctity, why institute the prayer of kedushah especially for the synagogue? It would therefore seem quite certain that during prayer the bibli-

[2] *Ibid.,* p. 124.

cal laws about holiness apply to the synagogue. Frivolity during the prayer would then be proscribed by the Scripture.

Necessarily, the Scriptural law must further apply to any occasion where people gather. For it is derived from the verse, "And the land shall mourn, every family apart: the family of the house of David apart, and their wives apart" (Zechariah 12:12), which indicates that men and women should be separate. Nowhere do we find that this instance of future mourning is to be in the Sanctuary . . . It therefore indicates that wherever men and women must gather they are forbidden to be without a dividing mechitzah between them, so that they cannot reach a state of levity. . . . And so in our synagogues, too, where people gather to pray, there must be a mechitzah, and it must be such that a mood of frivolity is quite out of question.

Thus nowadays, in a synagogue where men and women gather to pray, the ideal mechitzah remains a balcony, with women on the upper level. But if it is not feasible to build a balcony, a physical separation in the full sense of the term must be created so as to rule out any possible frivolity.

Prayer requires special concentration as well as a detachment from all distractions. Anything that might prevent this required concentration or provide an alternate focus of concentration is forbidden. Rambam reflects this idea in his work, *Hilchot Tefillah* 5:5, "And in all places one should not hold tefillin in his hand or a Torah in his arm and pray because his mind is preoccupied with them. Nor should he hold objects or money in his hand." Even things that make one self-conscious while praying are forbidden. Hence one cannot pray in front of a mirror. Rabbi Aaron Kotler[3] expounded on this theme:

> It is generally known that the most important part of prayer is sincerity and purity of thought, as it is expressed in Sifre and the Gemara [Talmud] (Taanith 2a): on the verse, "To serve Him with all your heart" (Deut. 11:13), they comment that this means prayer; and according to Maimonides it is a positive

[3] *Ibid.*, pp. 131–132.

commandment of the Torah. Now, "with all your heart" denotes that all one's powers and desires should be subordinated to prayer; the Sages interpret "with all your heart" to mean "with both your wills"—both the will to do good and the will to do evil should be subordinated to the service of the Lord.

This is expressly stated in numerous places in the writings of our early Sages.

Nothing is as disturbing to prayer as indecent thoughts, which render the prayers impure and unacceptable before the Lord. And how much more unacceptable is prayer when people incite their evil desires by deliberately seating men and women together, in contradiction to the laws and traditions of our nation. This is pure willfulness, which might bring about improper sights and improper thoughts. Beside the fact that this is in itself a serious transgression, it is even more contemptible when it takes place in the Palace of the King of Kings, the holy synagogue. According to the Law such people are not fulfilling their obligation in praying or in reading the Shema; all is voided and unacceptable before the Lord. In addition, whenever the name of God is uttered at such services, it is uttered in vain.

Yalkut Shim'oni (1,934) cites the Seder Eliyahu: "A man should not pray among women" because as the commentary there explains, he may be distracted by them. It has been stated by the foremost rabbinical authorities that a person should pray alone at home even on Rosh Hashanah and Yom Kippur rather than pray in a synagogue where men and women are not separated by a proper partition. Even if he must miss hearing the shofar or the reading of the Megillah on Purim, he should still pray at home rather than attend a synagogue that is not conducted according to law.

The sex drive is a strong and subtle aspect of the male personality. The comeliness of women is so attractive that it is distractive. It is too much to expect of a man sitting in feminine company to wholly devote himself and concentrate on praying to the Lord. One simply cannot expect a man's heart to be with God when his eyes are attracted elsewhere. After all, men are human beings—not angels. The sages recognize both the strengths and weaknesses of men. Women, too, will find it hard to concentrate on their prayer and feel the presence of God and be attracted to Him when they may be attracted to some men in their company.

Men and women are separated during prayer for a number of reasons, the most important of which is prevention of sexual distraction. Many areas of the Jewish Law take this fact into consideration. The separation of the sexes was introduced as an aid for us to be able to concentrate fully on our prayers and to call our God "out of the depth" of our hearts. A woman's presence not only provides the male with an alternate focus of attention but also makes him more self-conscious, thus preventing him from concentrating intensely on his prayers. While praying, we are to "know before Whom you stand," and not "know next to whom you are sitting."

A question relating to women and prayer is the question of a *minyan* (quorum for public prayer). Praying with a *minyan* is not a clearly defined obligation, even for men. The Rambam in *Hilchot Tefillah* 8:4–6 enumerates the parts of prayer that can only be conducted with a *minyan* (i.e. *Kedushah,* Torah reading, priestly blessings, etc.). Thus, he does not clarify whether men are obligated to pray with a *minyan* at all possible times. However, there are many rabbinic statements that encourage praying with a *minyan.*

Are women required to pray with a quorum? Can they be included in the quorum to make up the minimum number of people required for such purposes?

According to the Jewish Law, a *minyan* consists of ten adult males. This concept, discussed in the Talmud Megillah 23b, is derived from the verse, "How long shall I bear with this evil assembly. . . ?" (Num. 14:27). The term "assembly" here referred to the ten (male) spies who returned from scouting the Promised Land with an unfavorable report.

Since the term "assembly" used by the Torah referred to ten adult males, the Talmud concludes that for all matters requiring a congregation, ten adult males are necessary. It therefore follows that women are not obligated to pray with a *minyan* (they may join the services but cannot be counted toward making up a minyan). Thus, the ineligibility of women to be included in a minyan is a biblical injunction derived from the term "assembly" which was applied to ten adult males in a context. As such, it is not a form of discrimination but rather yet another instance of the Jewish Law's recognition of role differentiation concerning obligations for men and women. Women are certainly vital, essential, and indispensable members of the Jewish nation. Their not being eligible to take part in a male minyan has no bearing on their status as Jews.

A related question would be: Can women form their own minyan to recite those portions of prayers which require men to do so? In Orah Hachaim 55:1, it is clearly stated that women cannot be counted towards a minyan for any matter of holiness. This is based on the Talmud Berachot 45b and the Tosfot there. According to the Talmud, ten women are counted as ten individuals, and not as one group. This means if a group of ten women gather together to pray, they may not publicly recite the *Kaddish, Kedushah Borch-hu,* the thirteen divine attributes, and any other portion of rituals or prayers that require a minyan of ten adult males.

Besides the sources cited above, halachic authorities point to various other reasons for the unacceptability of minyan by women. Some authorities regard the women's minyan as an intimation of the ways of other nations, an act clearly forbidden by the Torah. In our present society, there exists an obsession (sometimes carried to absurd extremes) to prove men and women are equal in every imaginable aspect of life. The ideas of mixed prayer groups or women's prayer groups are yet other instances reflecting this belief and, as such, unacceptable by Torah standards. We simply do not believe that men and women can be equated in every aspect of life. Though it is a firm principle of Judaism that men and women are of equal importance, they nevertheless each hold uniquely separate obligations and responsibilities. Thus, the Code of Jewish Law does not sanction women's minyan.

According to halachic authorities, the idea of women's minyan is not compatible with two widely known principles. The first is a principle used throughout the Talmud: "In the multitude of people is the King's glory..." (Proverbs 14:28) (See Talmud Berachot 53a; Yoma 26a and 70a; Succah 52b; Rosh Hashanah 32b; Megillah 27b; Zebahim 14b; Menahot 62a.) Our rabbis learned from this verse that it is highly desirable to pray in a large synagogue where a large number of people gather for this purpose. This principle further indicates a sense of community orientation and cohesiveness—that the Jewish nation is one nation with one God. Thus, establishing separate minyans for men and women can be seen as a contradiction of this very basic tenet in Judaism.

The second principle that comes to play is: "Do not separate yourself from the congregation" (Mishnah Abot 2:4; Talmud Tannit 11a). Here our rabbis learn that a person is not to separate himself from the community, especially when it comes to religious activities. This principle can be seen as a clear pronouncement of the cohesiveness of the Jewish community, with everyone obligated to share in its happiness and sorrows. As such, the principle promotes the idea of praying with a congregation rather than at home, alone. And once again, separate minyans for women would not be tenable.

Yet another principle enunciated in Talmud Yebamot 14a can be understood as a supplement to the above principle expressed in Mishnah Abot 2:4. This principle states, "You shall not make multiple different gatherings."

The Jewish nation is very much community-oriented; many of the precepts of the Torah simply cannot be fulfilled without group participation. We pray to our one God as one nation in unison—men and women together. Moses, our teacher, emphasized this fact in the very beginning by saying to Pharaoh, "With our young and with our old, will we go, with our sons and with our daughters, . . . for we must hold a feast to the Lord" (Exod. 10:9).

As mentioned previously, many of the laws in Judaism were designed to prevent immorality before it occurs, and at its very onset. Therefore, a woman's voice (singing) is considered morally disturbing, for it is written: "Sweet is your voice and your countenance is comely" (Song of Songs 2:14). Based on this verse, the Talmud Berachot 24a (also mentioned in Kiddushin 70a) formulates that קל באשה ערוה "A woman's voice is provocative." Rashi comments that because the verse praises her for her voice, it is apparent that this makes her desirable.

Another way of understanding the verse is as follows: As established in the preceding chapters, modesty is a much cherished characteristic in Judaism, particularly as it pertains to women. Yet when a woman sings in the presence of a man, she also exposes her inner emotions and feelings—an act clearly contradictory to the basic Jewish principles of chastity and modesty. "The woman desires in her heart, and the man desires by speech, and this is a good characteristic among women" (Erubin 100b).

One may ask: How could the prophetess Deborah sing in public? *Seridi Eish* vol. II, no. 8 suggests that this involved no prohibition since her song of victory was divinely instructed and inspired. Another explanation is that she was singing the song simultaneously with a male companion, Barak ben Avinoam, and we have a principle that two individual voices cannot be heard simultaneously.

But then why is it that a man's singing voice is not considered morally disturbing to women, nor is it considered to make men more attractive? In Talmud Niddah 31b the sages comment: Why is a woman's voice sweet and a man's voice not sweet? Man derives his from the place from which he was created (i.e. the earth, which produces no resonant sound when it is pounded—Rashi); a woman derives hers from the place from which she was created (i.e. the bone, when one beats with it, resonant sounds can be produced—Rashi). Therefore, it can be assumed that a woman's singing voice intrinsically adds to her attractiveness and desirability to men, whereas a man lacks this intrinsic attraction for women. Hence, if Jewish law prohibits men from listening to the songs of a woman (Orah Hachaim 75:3; Even Ha-Ezer 21:1), it is not because women do not sing well, but rather because their attractive voices may be construed as seductive and cause men to think indecent thoughts. And, as we learn from an opinion in Talmud Yoma 29a, indecent thoughts are worse than committing the sin itself.

Rambam, in *Sefer Hamitzvot,* on negative commandment 353, states:

> We are warned against approaching any of the 'arayot' (women prohibited to us in marriage) even short of intercourse, as by embracing, or kissing, or other similar acts, as it is said, "None of you shall approach to any that is near of kin to him, to uncover their nakedness" (Lev. 18:6). As if He had said you shall not approach through any nearness that might lead to forbidden union.

Similarly, it is stated in Talmud Abodah Zarah 20b that a man is forbidden to gaze upon the nice clothes of a woman whom he knows, even if she is not wearing them at the time. Then surely it is forbidden if the woman is wearing them. The reason, as explained by Rambam (*Hilchot Issurei Bi'ah* 21:2) and in Shulchan Aruch Even ha-Ezer 21:1, is that such gazing would bring one to have indecent thoughts, for the Torah says: "And your camp shall be holy, that He shall not see in you any unseeming thing" (Deut. 23:15). Furthermore, Tosfot on Sanhedrin 20a states that it is a disgrace to the daughters of Israel if men gaze upon them.

One may ask—but don't women have feelings too? Can't they come to have indecent thoughts as well? Yes, women, too, have feelings that are on par with men, if not stronger. However, as Rabbi Ovadiah Yosef writes in his responsa (Yabia Omer 1 Orah Hachaim 6:5), we need not worry about women, since they are not בנות הרגשה (sensuous). It is understood that women have an easier time controlling their sexual feelings. According to Shulchan Aruch, Yoreh Deah 195:15–16, if a man is sick, his wife who is *niddah* (menstruating—this term will be defined more precisely later on) may nurse him and take care of his needs. However, if a woman who is *niddah* is sick, her husband may not care for her unless there are grave extenuating circumstances, lest he be unable to control his urges and come to have relations with her during her forbidden time.

[The observant reader might suspect a contradiction as earlier in the book it was stated that women are "light-minded," citing the incident of Bruriah's yielding to the repeated seductive attempts of Rabbi Meir's student. The "light-minded" statement, however, referred to circumstances where women are subjected to intense pressure or beguiled. Here, the reference is to normal, ordinary circumstances with an absence of undue pressure. In such instances, women have an easier time controlling their emotions and thoughts.]

As far as prayer is concerned, women definitely need to concentrate as much as men, and separation of the sexes exists for their sake as well. In terms of regular day-to-day life, it is true that women may come to have indecent thoughts as often as men, but they are also better able to control their feelings. The Jewish law stipulates special rules for both men and women in order to protect them even from indecent thoughts which might, eventually, lead to grave sins.

3
Family Purity

Torah law permeates all aspects of our lives; there is no time and no place void of God's presence ". . . the whole world is full of His glory" (Isaiah 6:3). The omnipresence of God is one of the most basic tenets of the Jewish faith, as attested by King David: "Where can I go from Your spirit? And where can I flee from Your presence? If I ascend to heaven, You are there. If I make my bed in the Lower World, behold it is You. Were I to take up wings of dawn, were I to dwell in the distant west, there, too, Your hand would guide me, and Your right hand shall grasp me" (Ps. 139:7–10). The function of Jewish law is to introduce the presence of God into all our daily activities, and establish a Jewish moral system. Thus the physical relationship between husband and wife, though a private and personal one, is governed by the laws of family purity which introduces the Divine Presence to this aspect of our lives. As Raavad understands it:[1]

> And so that man should know that there is a God who rules over him, He has set for him laws and restrictions in his relationship with his wife, as He set for him laws and restrictions in all other gifts that he has been given. If He has given man a field, He has commanded him on the plowing, the planting,

[1] Raavad, *Baal ha-Nefesh* (Jerusalem: Mosad Harav Kook), 1964, p. 15.

and the reaping. If He has given him food, He has set restrictions and commanded him concerning eating.

If He has given him clothing, He has commanded him also about its wearing. Even on man's body God set His sign with the covenant of circumcision. He has set limits on man's time by commanding him with the laws of Sabbath and Holidays. Also, to the gift of marriage He has given commandments and has tested man and commanded him to separate from his wife at certain times.

Briefly, Jewish Law forbids a husband and wife to have any physical contact during the woman's menstrual period (for five to seven days) and for another seven days thereafter. "And if a woman has an issue so that blood flows from her flesh, she shall be a *niddah* for seven days . . ." (Lev. 15:19). During this period, husband and wife are forbidden any physical expression of love, but are expected to treat each other with respect and affection. "You shall not approach a woman who is forbidden as a niddah to be intimate with her" (Lev. 18:19). During all this time, the woman is considered *niddah,* "impure." At the end of this period, the woman must immerse herself in a body of natural water such as a well or lake or rain-water (and not a pool or bath), known as a *mikvah.*

The term "impurity" used in connection with a woman who is a niddah, is not a precise term. Rabbi Norman Lamm,[2] in his book *A Hedge of Roses,* gives a clear explanation of this term. He understands "impurity" as an "intimation of death." A priest who comes in contact with a corpse becomes "impure." Even loss of potential life renders one "impure." For example, a leper who suffers from dying of the limbs is considered as if he were dead, and thus "impure." A man who suffers from running issue is "impure." If the issue is semen, it represents a loss of poten-

---

[2] Rabbi Norman Lamm, *A Hedge Of Roses* (Feldheim Publishers, 5th Ed., New York, 1977), pp. 81-91.

tial life; if the issue is in the form of pus, it afflicts the reproductive organ which is a source of life. Similarly, a woman who is niddah has lost an unfertilized ovum, a source of potential life, and so becomes "impure."

Water is a source of life. The human embryo, in its early stages, is about 95 percent water; the adult's total bodyweight is 60-70 percent water. As one ages, the water content of the body diminishes, ". . . as though the water content of the body were a measure of its vital activity. It would appear that the flame of life is sustained by water." Therefore, "impurity," "the intimation of death," of any origin is counteracted by immersion in the waters of the *mikvah*, the symbol of life.

Before immersing herself in the mikvah, the wife makes a blessing thanking God for sanctifying us through this institution, and thereby acknowledges, in a symbolic manner, that the husband and wife's relationship is sanctified and blessed—holy, not lecherous. Rabbi Lamm adds the following enlightening comments on the meaning of family purity:[3]

> It purifies and ennobles the outlook of man and woman upon each other and their relationship to each other. The very waters of the mikvah seem to wash away any fallacious, psychologically damaging thought which, carryovers from youth, may well imperil the mutual love and respect that alone can keep a home stable. Mikvah becomes the sacred instrumentality whereby morality and sexuality are reconciled, bringing husband and wife to each other in purity and delicacy, their love undefiled by the guilt and shame that are the relics of obsolete inner struggles.

Rabbi S. R. Hirsch in his commentary on Lev. 18:19[4] reinforces the above idea by writing: "Apart from deep

---

[3] *Ibid.*, pp. 38-39.

[4] Rabbi S. R. Hirsch, *The Pentateuch* (Judaica Press, LTD. Gateshead, 1982), p. 489.

physiological reasons, which surely prevail here too, no law more than this, raises sexual intercourse out of the sphere of lower sensuality into the realm of morally pure, sanctified humanity."

A further clarification of the term "impurity" is in order. This term by no means ascribes any intrinsic, mysterious abhorrence to the menstruating woman who could, in turn, be purified by some magical means. Neither is it meant to lower the person so labled to an inferior status. The terms "pure" and "impure" signify purely halachic or legal categories. They indicate that in each case certain patterns of behavior become obligatory. A striking example is the order of the service and rituals performed by the High Priest in the Holy Temple on Yom Kippur. Even though involved in holy services in the most holy place on earth, the High Priest was considered "impure" after each stage of sacrificial service and was required to change his clothing and immerse himself in water before going on to the next stage of the service.

Another vivid example is the ceremony of the sacrifice of the red heifer. The ashes of the red heifer would render those who came in contact with it "pure" if they were in a state of "impurity;" and "impure" if they were in a state of "purity" (that is, the priest who performed the ceremony and all other "pure" people who came in contact with the ashes). The reason(s) for these laws are beyond our understanding. In fact, in the Talmud Yoma 14a and Niddah 9a, with regard to the laws of purity and impurity, the Talmud relates the comment of King Solomon, the wisest of all men, "All this have I proved by wisdom, I said I will be wise; but it was far from me" (Ecclesiastes 7:23).

The Hebrew root for the word *niddah* is *nadad,* meaning "separated" or "removed." Thus, the *state of niddah* means that the woman must be "removed" and "separated" from her husband. Hence, the word *niddah* connotes separation and does not even have the connotation of menstruation, let alone impurity.

Immersion in a mikvah is not for hygenic reasons. Surely it is not meant to remove any dirt, as a woman is required to thoroughly clean herself directly beforehand. There have been studies which indicate that Jewish women suffer less than non-Jewish women from cancer of the cervix, a fatal disease. And there is a lower incidence of urinary tract infection in Jewish men and women compared to non-Jews. Thus inferences have been made that such is the case because of the Jews' observance of the family purity laws. As true as these inferences might be, they could not have been the only concern of the halacha.

First and foremost, the laws of family purity serve as a reminder that there is no area of our lives from which the Divine Presence is absent. Another very important function of these laws is to strengthen the Jewish family structure. These laws serve to periodically separate couples, thus making each spouse more dear and causing them to look forward to getting together with greater enthusiasm and anticipation. The laws serve to prevent marital discord, as Rabbi Lamm writes, "Unrestricted approachability leads to over-indulgence. And this over-familiarity, with its consequent satiety and boredom and ennui, is a direct and powerful cause of marital disharmony." So also, by observing the laws, a monotonous marital relationship is averted.

Rabbi Meir in Talmud Niddah 31b emphasizes this endearment element in the laws of family purity by saying, "Why did the Torah say that a menstruating woman is forbidden to her husband for seven days? Because, since the husband becomes over-acquainted with his wife, he may begin to find her unpleasing. Therefore, the Torah said to let her be forbidden for seven days so that she will be as dear to her husband as the day of his marriage."

These laws also remind the couple not to treat each other as sexual objects or simply as a means of gratification. In a way, they make it possible for the couple to relate on a more human and non-sexual level. This also serves as an excellent training in consideration for every couple since there are often times when men and women cannot relate sexually, as when one is sick or not emotionally receptive to a sexual overture for whatever reason.

In conclusion, the laws of family purity are not meant to make women feel taboo or unclean, but rather are designed to elevate sex by enabling mates to relate to one another as people and not merely as sex objects. They were never intended to ostracize women or make them feel unclean. On the contrary. They force the couple to relate to one another as complete human beings rather than as objects for the satisfaction of sexual drives. The woman's monthly period is a God given gift to humanity; it serves to preserve the close and healthy relationship between husband and wife. By helping avoid monotony in marriage, the laws of family purity afford the couple a monthly honeymoon while making each partner dearer and more precious to the other. It is common during the course of a marriage for tensions to develop and problems to arise. The monthly physical separation of the husband and wife provides each an opportunity to learn to communicate on a non-physical level. After the woman immerses herself in the mikvah, it is as if their marriage is reborn, and the couple ready to make a new start.

The laws of family purity reflect a rhythm of intimacy and separation between man and woman corresponding to the times of the month when the potential for new life is most real, and when that potential is lost. They also ensure that even the most powerful of physical and emotional drives be touched with an awareness of holiness.

Thus, we again see how the observation of the fundamental laws of morality is so crucial to our existence and our survival, both as individuals and as a nation; and how minute details of these laws permeate, affect, and direct our personal lives.

Part Five
WOMEN AND REDEMPTION

Since its very inception, the Jewish nation was promised deliverance and redeemers. We have already experienced deliverance from Egypt and from subsequent enemies throughout history. We still await the final, perfect, and absolute deliverance, the coming of the Messiah. In the final part of this book, the connection between these deliverances, redeemers, and women is presented.

I
Jews and the Messianic Era

All Jews who accept the thirteen principles of faith believe there exists a personal Messiah who will come and for whom the nations of the earth should await. Article 12 affirms: "I believe with perfect faith in the coming of the Messiah, and although he may tarry, I wait daily for his coming." In accordance with this teaching, the Messiah will come and deliver the Jewish nation. He will reestablish the throne of David and introduce an era of peace and prosperity. During his reign, Israel shall be exalted to her Divinely appointed place at the head of the nations.

The idea of a redeemer is a very basic and ancient concept. In Genesis 3:15 we find: "And I [God] will put an enmity between your [the snake's] seed and between her seed, she shall bruise your head and you shall bruise her heel." Here the snake represents the "adversary," the one who caused Adam and Eve to sin. Taken allegorically, the adversaries are the nations of the world who through their corrupt cultures and perverse ways try to influence the children of Israel to sin against God. So, from early on, we see it promised that from the seed of Eve will come the redeemer who will dominate over evil and deliver Israel.

Lamech saw the coming of this future redeemer in a prophetic vision, and blended the description of the work that his son Noah would do with that of the Redeemer (Gen. 5:29).

At the time of his death, Jacob saw the situation of "the latter days" and foretold the rise of one from Judah who would receive the obedience of all nations. Furthermore, while blessing Dan, Jacob makes this puzzling plea: "For Your salvation I have waited, O' Lord" (Gen. 49:18). Rashi comments that Jacob prophesied that the Philistines would pull out Samson's eyes, and Samson, the redeemer of the Jews, would say, "Remember me, I pray to You, and strengthen me, I pray to You only this once" (Judges 16:28). However, the verse can also be interpreted as alluding to the long awaited salvation of all Jews, starting with our forefather Israel or Jacob.

Balaam was given a clear forecast of the earth's redemption from the curse, and of the star rising out of Jacob to whom world dominion would be assigned. "I see him, but not now, I behold him but not nigh, [there] shall step forth a star from Jacob and a scepter shall rise out of Israel" (Num. 24:17).

Channah, too, was granted a vision of the future. In her song of praise, she revealed the fact that all of the early predictions would be fulfilled in one who, for the first time, is called "the Messiah."

ה' ידין אפסי־ארץ ויתן־עז למלכו וירם קרן משיחו "The Lord will judge the ends of the earth, and He will grant strength to His King, and raise the horn of His anointed one (Messiah)" (I Samuel 2:10).

Finally, the end was clearly revealed to the prophet Daniel (as it was to Jacob), and the Book of Daniel embodies many of the prophecies about our future. The Midrash Schocher Tov 31:7 reports: "[Only] to two people did the Holy-One-Blessed-be-He reveal the End; to Jacob and to Daniel."

Embedded deep in every Jewish heart is a longing for the coming of the Messiah. In many quarters the ancient hope still burns as bright as ever. Every day, Jews conclude their daily prayers with *Alenu,* a prayer expressing our hope and desire for the coming of the Messianic period—for a time when the unity of God will be ubiquitous and His Kingdom of Justice and Peace will be established on earth.

2

Women's Intuition

We have already discussed a number of female prophets in our Tradition, starting all the way back with our mother, Sarah. At this point, however, the author would like to suggest that women in general possess a measure of prophecy. Some people might call it "women's sixth sense" or "insight." There is a Talmudic saying (Niddah 45b) that women possess בינה יתרה (*binah yeterah*) meaning, literally, "extra knowledge." Rabbi Chisda comments that this means women were given greater intelligence than men. The Ritba, however, understands *binah yeterah* as referring to a woman's earlier attainment of physical and intellectual maturity.

It is the author's humble opinion that *binah yeterah* refers to a Divinely endowed insight. Upon dreaming about "the end of the days," Daniel is very perplexed and seeks to understand what he has dreamt. He says: ואבקשה בינה "And I sought understanding" (Daniel 8:15). Here Daniel asks for a Divinely endowed understanding of what he has seen in his dream, and he uses the word *binah* in making his request.

The fact that *binah* refers to a sort of Divine insight can also be gleaned from the following. King David appealed to God with, אמרי האזינה ה' בינה הגיגי "To my sayings give ear, God, perceive my thoughts" (Ps. 5:2). According to Rashi, King David is appealing to God to perceive [through His *binah*, His Divine level of understanding] his thoughts which are sealed up in his heart because fear and worry have rendered him mute and incapable of putting his desires into words. Furthermore, when God asks Solomon what he desires, Solomon answers: ונתת לעבדך לב שמע לשפט את־עמך להבין בין־טוב לרע "Give Your servant an understanding heart to judge Your people, that I may discern between good and evil" (I Kings 3:9). Once again the term *binah* is employed when what is desired is a higher prophetic level of understanding.

Another instance of the word *binah* occurs in the blessing before the recitation of the Shema, a blessing in which men are obligated but women are exempt. The blessing reads: ותן בלבנו (בינה) להבין להשכיל לשמע ללמד וללמד "And put in our heart [understanding, according to the Sephardic version] to understand and to discern, to perceive, to learn and to teach." Thus we learn that every man—not only King Solomon, the wisest of all men, and not only Daniel the prophet—prays before the Lord to give him *binah*, meaning understanding in the form of that extra prophetic measure He has instilled in women.

Eliyahu Kitov is of a similar opinion. He writes:[1]

> Man and woman differ in understanding and insight as they do in nature. Men acquire understanding largely through social intercourse, men who are restricted to the confines of their homes have but a narrow understanding. But women find their insight largely within themselves. Indeed insights that are communicated to them from abroad often impair their natural insight. The difference is one between wisdom and insight. Wisdom derives from communication, insight follows from the self. In depth of insight, in intuition, the rabbis considered women superior to men.

---

[1] Eliyahu Kitov, *The Jew and His Home* (Shengold Publishers, Inc. 3rd Ed., N.Y. 1963), p. 35.

3
The Role of Women in Bringing Forth the Redeemers of the Jews

Many women were instrumental in bringing redeemer of Israel to the world. Sarah, through her Divinely endowed insight, knew prophetically that the redeemer of Israel would eventually come from her and Abraham's sons, Isaac. For this reason, she asked Abraham to cast out her maid Hagar and Hagar's son (fathered by Abraham), to ensure that nothing and nobody would interfere with the long chain of generations from Isaac to the redeemer.

Rebecca, in turn, advised her son Jacob to secure the blessings from his father, thus preventing Jacob's unworthy brother Esau from receiving the blessings and carrying on the tradition of the forefathers. Rebecca, like Sarah before her, saw through her Divinely endowed insight that the redeemer would come from Jacob, and hence acted in order to ensure this future event.

The story of Judah and Tamar is a puzzling one. In chapter 38 of Genesis we are told that Judah took a wife and begot three sons: Er, Onan, and Shelah. Judah married off his first-born, Er, to Tamar. Er died shortly afterwards, and Judah asked his second son, Onan, to marry Tamar. However Onan, too, died shortly after his marriage. Judah then sent Tamar back to her father's house saying to her ". . . till Shelah my son be grown up [to marry her]" (Gen. 38:11), but actually thinking to himself, ". . . lest he [Shelah] also die" (Ibid.).

A short time thereafter, Judah's wife died. Tamar soon realized that Judah was not going to keep his word and let Shelah marry her. When Judah went up to his sheep-shearers in Timnah, Tamar dressed herself as a prostitute and waited by the road for Judah. Judah, not recognizing his daughter-in-law and thinking she was an ordinary prostitute, had relations with her. (In those times, before the Torah was given, having relations with prostitutes was a permissible act.) Later on, Judah found out that the "prostitute" was really his daughter-in-law and that she had become pregnant by him. Tamar, however, did not publicly reveal the fact that Judah himself had relations with her, so that Judah would not be embarrassed in public. Then Judah declared, "She is more righteous than I" (Gen. 38:26).

Rashi comments on this incident by noting that our rabbis said a heavenly voice went forth and said, "By me and from me did [these] things come to pass. Because she was chaste in the house of her father-in-law, I decreed that kings shall issue from her, and from the tribe of Judah have I decreed to establish kings in Israel." From this episode our rabbis learn that one should never put someone to shame in public; just as Tamar tried to avoid publicly shaming Judah.

One may ask: Why was it so important to Tamar to beget a child from Judah? Torah Temimah, commenting upon ". . . and [Tamar] sat in the open eyes" (Gen. 38:14), says that she set her eyes to the place where all people hope, that is the house of Abraham, and she prayed to the Heavens not to be sent away empty-handed from that house.

The author would like to suggest that Tamar, too, through her special feminine insight, saw that the redeemer of Israel would come from the union of Judah and herself. Therefore, she prayed to God to help bring about such a union. Meam Loez on Genesis 38:16 states t[hat Judah was] ambivalent about approaching Tamar, but [God sent] His angel of lust, persuaded Judah to approach [the prosti]tute." As we read in the Book of Ruth, the fruit [of this uni]on eventually led to the birth of David from whom the Messiah is destined to descend.

Yet another woman of rare understanding and wisdom was Miriam the prophetess. After Pharaoh's decree to kill every boy born to the Jews, many Jewish couples separated, thinking to themselves that in this way they would avoid bringing children into the world who would face certain death. However, wise Miriam with her prophetic insight said to her parents, "You are worse than Pharaoh. He has decreed only against male children but you are condemning the female as well" (Rashi on Exod. 2:1). Subsequently, her parents reunited, and as a result Moses, the redeemer of the Children of Israel, was born.

In another instance both Miriam and her mother Yocheved demonstrated their superior bravery and their fear of God. When Pharaoh ordered them, as midwives, to kill every son born to a Jewish woman, not only did they not kill any baby born to an Israelite, but they continued to help deliver the Jewish babies so that Israel shall not be deprived of her redeemer (Moses). Because of their bravery and faith in God, they were rewarded: "And since the midwives feared God, He made them houses" (Exod. 1:21). Rashi explains (see also Sotah 12a) that the "Houses of *Kehuna* and *Leviah*" (the priests and the Levites) will come from Yocheved, and the "House of Royalty" (the future kings and royals) will descend from Miriam.

The quote, "By the merit of righteous women our fathers were redeemed from Egypt" (Sotah 11b) was mentioned at the beginning of this book.

The story of Channah, also presented earlier, serves as yet another vivid example of how our redemption came through our women. Why was Channah so dissatisfied?

After all, her husband loved her dearly despite the fact that she was barren. Here again, the author would like to suggest that Channah knew something of which her husband was unaware. Through her measure of prophecy, Channah knew that Israel would be led through the actions of her son Samuel, who would also serve to anoint Saul and then David as kings, "... and raise the horn of His anointed one" (I Samuel 2:10). And it was because of such knowledge that she earnestly prayed to the Lord to give her the merit of mothering this future celebrated prophet of Israel.

It also happened that when agents of King Saul were out to kill David, David's wife, Michal, saved him, thereby keeping intact the long chain to the Messiah.

Ruth serves as another example of a valiant woman who kept the chain intact. Why was Ruth so intent on leaving the land of her fathers to dwell in a strange country where life would be miserable compared to the royal life she was accustomed to leading in her hometown? Why did she long to marry Boaz? Ruth, with the counsel of her mother-in-law Naomi, approached Boaz through cunning, saying, "... spread your robe over your handmaid; for you are a redeemer" (Ruth 3:9). One may conjecture that Ruth, through her Divinely endowed insight, knew that the Messiah was destined to come from her union with Boaz. As we learn from the genealogy presented at the end of the Book of Ruth, Boaz was the great-grandfather of David, from whose line is destined to come the Messiah. The sages teach in Baba Basra 91b that Ruth enjoyed unusual longevity. She lived to see her royal descendent Solomon ascend the throne.

When the wicked Haman planned to kill all the Jews in the Persian Empire, Esther and Mordechai arrived on the scene to save them. Queen Esther did not forget her people while she lived in the palace of King Ahashverosh, and came to risk her life in order to save the Jewish nation from annihilation. Esther's words to the King were, "Let my life be given me at my petition, and my people at my request" (Megillath Esther 7:3). She then directed her eyes heavenward, "... and if I then perish, I perish" (Ibid. 4:16). As we see, Esther was ready to sacrifice her own life in an attempt to spare the lives of her fellow Jews.

Each of the above women did her part to ensure the eventual coming of the Messiah, our final redeemer. It is clear that women have played, and continue to play, a vital role in Judaism; and are known to occupy a very high status position within our Tradition. Women are considered the source of everything good that is to be found in our world in general, and in the world of Judaism, in particular. They are the true "Invaluable Pearl."

Eve was the mother of all living beings; Sarah, the mother of prophecy; Miriam, the mother of deliverance; the women of the generation of the exodus, mothers of pure faith; Deborah, the mother of heroism; Ruth, the mother of royalty; Esther, the mother of redemption. And the righteous and virtuous Jewish women of our own time are the mothers of the Messianic era. With this let us pray for the coming of our true and righteous Messiah soon, and in our times, Amen. Let the vision of Isaiah be realized: "And I will bring [them] to My Holy Mountain, and make them joyful in My House of Prayer; their burnt-offerings and their sacrifices shall be accepted upon My altar; for My House shall be called a house of prayer for all the nations" (Isaiah 56:7). So that, "The Lord shall be King over all the earth; on that day the Lord shall be One and His name One" (Zechariah 14:9).

Afterword

Throughout this book, we have often tried to explain concepts or laws according to their underlying reasons. However, it should be pointed out that the Holy laws of the Torah are well beyond human comprehension. The Torah says, "The secret things belong unto the Lord our God, but the things that are revealed belong to us and to our children forever, that we may do all the words of this Torah" (Deut. 29:28). We do know that we are considered children of the Lord: "You are children of the Lord your God" (Deut. 14:1). And we are assured that, "The Lord your God loves you" (Deut. 23:6). Therefore, our first reaction to the commandments of our God should be the same as that of our forefathers upon receiving the Torah: נעשה ונשמע, "We do and [then] hear [understand]."

We know that our Father in Heaven always desires what is best for us and that, therefore, our obedience to Him is actually for our own good. This same idea is reflected in the wise words of King Solomon, "Trust in God with your whole heart and do not lean upon your own understanding. In all your ways acknowledge Him, and he will direct your paths aright" (Proverbs 3:5–6).

Rambam (*Hilchot Meilah* 8:8), however, stressed the importance of searching for underlying principles, but he issued a word of caution:

It is fitting for a man to ponder the laws of the holy Torah and to comprehend their full meaning to the extent of his full ability. Nevertheless, a law for which he finds no reason and for which he sees no cause should not be trivial in his eyes. Let him not "break forth to rise up against the Lord, lest the Lord break forth upon him," (paraphrase of Exod. 19:21,22), and let him not think about the Torah in the same manner as he thinks about secular and everyday matters. Let us see how strict the Torah was with the crime of Meilah [the crime of using for one's own personal use an object that has been designated for use in the service of the Temple]. Now, if wood and stones, earth and ashes, just because a man has designated them for use in the Temple, by speech alone have become sanctified and anyone who treats them in an ordinary everyday manner has committed the crime of Meilah, and even if he did this unintentionally he requires atonement, how much more should a man be on guard not to rebel against a commandment decreed for us by the Almighty, only because he does not understand the reason, nor should he ascribe incorrect things to God, nor should he regard the commandments as ordinary affairs.

If one searches for and ascribes underlying moral purposes to the commandments of God, it should not be done for the purpose of judging the Divine Law, but rather to strengthen and to deepen one's own understanding. Rabbi Samson Raphael Hirsch echoes this view in his commentary on Psalms:[1]

> Such speculation and attempts at inquiry into motives behind these laws would be a presumptuous and dangerous undertaking for a person who does not cleave to God's commandments simply because they are His, but who makes his belief in their sanctity and binding force subject to the result of his investigation into their reason and purposes. Such inquiry on the part of him in whose heart אמונה במצות ה' emunah be'mitzvot hashem [commitment to mitzvot of God] does not take precedence over

---

[1] in the introduction to chapter 119 (New York, Feldheim Publishers 1966).

his speculation upon them would be a fatal venture indeed. It should be remembered that a person of this morality is not led to defection through his speculation, for he has already set aside the אמונה במצות emunah be'mitzvot [commitment to mitzvot] long before he has ever crossed the threshold to the hall of thought and inquiry. The request in this psalm for better understanding and insight, therefore bases itself upon an avowal in the words כי האמנתי במצותיך kee he'amanti be'mitzvoteckha [for I am committed to your mitzvot]; his אמונה במצותיך emunah bemitzvotekha [commitment to Your mitzvot] is not to be based upon such insight and understanding, but should precede the latter and form the granite foundation for whatever investigation he might undertake. The sole reason why he seeks to inquire into the word of God is that, to him, the divine commandments are indeed the law of the Lord, and hence by inquiring into them, he seeks to investigate the trial of the Divine wisdom, even as the human mind endeavors to search the marvels of nature and history for the demonstration of God's wisdom and almighty power. And he prays: גל עיני ואביט נפלאות מתורתיך gal aynai ve'abitah niflaot mi'Toratekha "Open Thou my eyes, that I may behold miracles from Thy Law," (Ps. 119:18).

Rabbi Abraham R. Besdin in his book *Reflections of the Rav*,[2] which is an adaptation of thoughts expressed by Rabbi Joseph B. Soloveitchik, expresses a similar view. He writes that the Kabbalist taught us that man is endowed with two wills. Man's *ratzon elyon* (higher will), not his rationality, "... constitutes the singular endowment which distinguishes him from the rest of the creation." This will, autonomous of the intellect, effects man's major decisions in life. "Decisions of faith, of marriage, choice of profession, solutions to financial problems, acts of military genius, and most pivotal resolutions in life are reached intuitively, without addressing any inquiries to the intellect. Without *ratzon elyon*, great minds would never have made their revolution-

[2] Jewish Agency, Jerusalem 1979, pp. 91–98.

ary discoveries in science, religion, and other fields." As can be seen from the words of the great genius of the twentieth century, Albert Einstein:[3] "At times I feel certain that I am right without knowing the reason. When the eclipse of 1919 confirmed my intuition, I was not in the least surprised."

The other will is man's intellect, ". . . which weighs pros and cons, is of subordinate stature in man's personality and is called *ratzon tachton,* the lower, practical will." Rabbi Soloveitchik acknowledges the fact that science is needed to unravel the mysteries of nature, and that logic is used to arrive at rational concepts. However, ". . . we rely on an inner illumination (*ratzon elyon*) to answer pivotal questions."

But these two wills (*ratzon elyon* and *ratzon tachton*) are often in conflict. Rabbi Soloveitchik feels that one is to give precedence to *ratzon elyon,* and that this does not imply belittlement of the intellect. "Indeed man is bidden in the Bible to use his mind in order to achieve dominion over nature, and, in effect, to combat disease and poverty. The Talmud employs logical analysis in its deliberations, searching for underlying principles and applying them to diverse situations. The intellectual emphasis has always been a distinctive characteristic of the Jewish life." However, man is to understand that his intellect is not unlimited, ". . . it has boundaries within which it exercises its cognitive powers." Therefore, *ratzon tachton* should not take precedence over *ratzon elyon.* This is a very important principle in Judaism. ". . . without the *ratzon elyon* the Jew could not sustain his commitments to the demanding discipline of mitzvot observance and the unshakable faith in our people's future."

The following parable illustrates how using one's *ratzon tachton* (intellect) and ignoring one's *ratzon elyon* (intuition) can lead to unfortunate events.

The Torah commands that a Jewish king shall not take too many wives, not amass too much wealth, and not acquire

---
[3] *Cosmic Religion,* p. 7.

more horses than he needs. The wise King Solomon rationalized that since he knew the reason for these commandments (that one should not be led astray from devotion to God) he could be careful and need not obey them. Thus King Solomon took many wives, amassed an incredible amount of wealth, and acquired many horses. Later we find in I Kings chapter 11 that Solomon, under the influence of his foreign wives, came to sin against God by overlooking his wives' idol worship. The Scripture says of him, "And Solomon did what was displeasing to the Lord, and he was not completely devoted to the Lord as was David his father" (I Kings 11:6). In Talmud Sanhedrin 21b Rabbi Yitzhak concludes that the reasons for the commandments were not revealed since when the reason for two commandments (not to take too many wives, not to have too many horses) was revealed, even a man of King Solomon's stature (through rationalization) infringed upon them.

Therefore, since we cannot begin to fathom the depth of reasons for God's commandments and His grand plan for the world, it is in our best interest to observe His commandments as He commanded us, "To keep the commandments of the Lord and His statutes which I [Moses] command you this day for your good" (Deut. 10:13).

It is interesting to note that from the moment of birth there exists a dichotomy between male and female. From the very moment of delivery, it is understood that the male has to strive to get closer to God, he must work to achieve spiritual height. For instance, as a mere infant, he is to be circumcised, thereby entering the covenant of God and Israel. But could not God have created the male so that there would be no need for circumcision? As it is written: "Is anything too hard for the Lord?" (Gen. 18:14). Surely there is nothing beyond the power of the Almighty. And He is the only One who knows the actual reasons for all His commandments.

Let us now review some of the key concepts presented in this book. It is hoped that the reader will be able to use these concepts along with the rest of the contents to resolve questions or issues that are not addressed in the book.

(A) Men and women are not equal; however, neither one is superior or inferior to the other in an absolute sense, provided each follows the commandment of the Lord and the rabbinic enactments. Man and woman are like king and queen, but each rules in a different world. Each sex has different roles, and therefore different rights and obligations. Thus, both man and woman must realize and abide by their role differentiation, their privileges, and their restrictions. Although women do have a small edge over men in some areas—for example, they are one step closer to God in their faith and devotion to Him; men can reach that same level of spiritual height through the observance of God's commandments, particularly those commandments from which women are exempt.

(B) Modesty is a deeply appreciated trait in Judaism and is expected to be found in Jewish women in particular. As medieval Jewish writers wrote, "The noblest of all ornaments is modesty. Modesty is humility and wisdom combined. A small act done modestly is thousandfold more acceptable to God than a big act done in pride."

Man is like the trunk of a tree, the visible and public part of the plant. Although his activities are broad, visible, and out in the open, they are also short-lasting. Woman, on the other hand, is like the roots of a tree, invisible and private. Her activities may be more limited and secluded, but they are long-lasting. Thus, a woman's role is primarily defined within the private domain. However, as needs arise, and within the framework and spirit of the Jewish law, women may participate in activities beyond their usual private sphere. The women described in Part One of this book and the אשת חיל, "Woman of Valor" serve as excellent role models for today's women who are active both inside and outside the home.

(C) Man and woman were created to be בשר אחד, a functioning unit, they are meant to be one soul in two bodies, and to do the will of the Almighty. Together they can reach the highest levels of spirituality and fulfillment in life.

(D) The most important concept discussed is that the survival of the Jews and Judaism depends on absolute faith in God, and obeying His will. We are—each one of us—to proclaim again, as we proclaimed at Mount Sinai when the Torah was first given to us: נעשה ונשמע—we will first do God's will and then try to understand His reasons. And we are to stay away from the corrupt, earthly, inconsequential practices and activities of the other nations around us. In the wise words of King Solomon, סוף דבר הכל נשמע את־האלהים ירא ואת מצותיו שמור כי זה כל האדם "The end of the matter is, let us hear the whole: Fear God, and keep His commandments, for this is the whole [duty of] man" (Ecclesiastes 12:13).

Index

Abraham, 3, 4, 7, 77, 87, 105, 171, 179
Achish, 55
Agunah, 133, 134, 135
Akiba, 27, 36, 37, 38, 68
Aknai Oven, 23
Baba ben Buta, 68
Bath Sheva, 146
Bruriah, 31, 33, 34, 35, 109, 111, 158
Candles, 17, 98, 103
Career, 73, 74
Challah, 103
Channah, 10, 11, 61, 113, 168, 173, 174
Chanukah, 16, 17, 18, 86, 98
Circumcision, 101, 160, 181
Contract, 129, 130
Credibility, 121, 122, 123, 124, 126
Deborah, 9, 10, 11, 156, 175
Derogatory, 27, 28
Divine Presence, 24, 25, 62, 68, 69
Domination, 76
Economic, 25
Eli, 11
Esau, 4, 171
Esther, 14, 15, 86, 98, 174
Evil Inclination, 146, 147, 149
Evil wife, 30, 80
Fear of God, 7, 108, 110
Futility, 71, 72
Golden calf, 6, 87, 140
Hagar, 3, 171
Halitzah, 135
Hamta, 35
Hell, 28, 29, 30
Huldah, 13
Ima Shalom, 32, 33, 34, 35

Impurity, 160, 161, 162
Isaac, 4, 171
Ishmael, 3, 27
Jacob, 4, 5, 7, 31, 61, 69, 88, 111, 168, 171
Jezebel, 29
Joseph, 5, 31, 37, 179
Kabbalah, 45
Ketubah, 129, 130, 132, 133
Kimchit, 49
Kiyor, 6
Leah, 5, 61, 67, 78
Lulab, 86, 90, 96, 102
Maccabee, 17
Mechitzah, 148, 149, 150, 151
Messiah, 16, 167, 168, 174, 175
Michal, 91, 174
Mikvah, 7, 103, 160, 161, 163
Minyan, 153, 154, 155
Miriam, 5, 173, 175
Mordechai, 14, 174
Naomi, 15, 16, 174
On ben Peleth, 79, 80
Orpah, 15
Passover, 6, 7, 86, 98, 101, 117
Physician, 28, 29, 147
Political, 25
Purim, 15, 86, 98, 152
Rachel, 4, 5, 37, 38, 61, 78
Rebecca, 4, 60, 67, 78, 171
Ritzpah, 12, 13
Rosh Hodesh, 7
Ruth, 15, 16, 174
Sarach, 5
Sarah, 3, 4, 47, 48, 60, 67, 77, 78, 87, 111, 171, 175
Saul, 13, 54, 91
Secular, 71, 110

Sexual, 44, 76, 103, 127, 153, 162, 164
Shofar, 86, 90, 102
Slaves, 116, 117, 118, 122, 124, 134
Succah, 72, 86, 90, 96
Taboo, 164
Tamar, 16, 67, 171, 172, 173
Tiflut, 106, 108
Witchcraft, 30

Woman of Valor, 62, 182
Yael, 10
Yehudit, 18, 98
Yoab, 12
Yocheved, 173
Yoharah, 94, 95
Yom Kippur, 86, 98, 152, 162
Zelophehad, 7, 8